Edward Taylor

Revised Edition

Twayne's United States Authors Series

Patricia Cowell, Editor

Colorado State University

TUSAS 8

From George Wither, *A Collection of Emblemes, Ancient and Moderne: Quickened with Metrical Illustrations, both Morall and Divine: And Disposed into Lotteries, that Instruction, and Good Counsell, may bee furthered by an Honest and Pleasant Recreation* (London, 1635).

Edward Taylor

Revised Edition

By Norman S. Grabo

The University of Tulsa

Twayne Publishers
A Division of G. K. Hall & Co. • Boston

Edward Taylor, Revised Edition
Norman S. Grabo

Copyright 1988 by G.K. Hall & Co.
All rights reserved.
Published by Twayne Publishers
A Division of G.K. Hall & Co.
70 Lincoln Street
Boston, Massachusetts 02111

Copyediting supervised by Barbara Sutton
Book production by Gabrielle B. McDonald
Book design by Barbara Anderson

Typeset in 11 pt. Garamond
by Huron Valley Graphics, Inc., Ann Arbor, Michigan

Printed on permanent/durable acid-free paper
and bound in the United States of America

Library of Congress Cataloging-in-Publication Data

Grabo, Norman S.
  Edward Taylor.

  (Twayne's United States authors series; TUSAS 8)
  Bibliography: p.
  Includes index.
  1. Taylor, Edward, 1642–1729—Criticism and
interpretation. 2. Christian literature, American—
History and criticism. I. Title. II. Series.
PS850.T2Z67   1988   811'.1   87-34991
ISBN 0-8057-7521-8 (alk. paper)

To Effie

Contents

About the Author

Norman S. Grabo received his B.A. at Elmhurst College (1952), his M.A. (1955) and Ph.D. (1958) from UCLA. He has taught English and American literature at Michigan State University (1958–63), the University of California at Berkeley (1963–77), Texas A&M University as Distinguished Professor (1977–83), and the University of Tulsa, where he is Chapman Professor of English. Between 1970 and 1975 he taught in the Great Books Program at St. John's College (Santa Fe). He has been awarded fellowships from the Folger Shakespeare Library, the Society for Religion in Higher Education, the Guggenheim Foundation, and the National Endowment for the Humanities.

The first version of this book, *Edward Taylor* (1961), was the first book-length study of Taylor. Grabo subsequently edited *Edward Taylor's Christographia* (1962), *Edward Taylor's Treatise Concerning the Lord's Supper* (1966), *American Thought and Writing* (with Russel B. Nye, 1965), and *American Poetry and Prose* (with Norman Foerster and others, 1970). He helped edit Charles Brockden Brown's *Arthur Mervyn* in the Bicentennial Edition (1980), published *The Coincidental Art of Charles Brockden Brown* (1981), and edited with an introduction the Penguin edition of Brown's *Edgar Huntly* (1988). In addition to lectures, presentations, and journal articles on a broad range of colonial topics, he is presently engaged in the preparation of a broad history of colonial American literature called "American Literary Design, 1520–1820."

Preface to the Revised Edition

Fifty years after the first serious publication of Edward Taylor's poetry and its first critical appraisal, Taylor has become a permanent fixture in American literature. Debates about the content of the American literary canon or the ideology and theory of American literary history only enhance and strengthen Taylor's stature. Like other genuine literary classics, his work yields to many critical tests without being reduced to irrelevance. In the quarter-century since this study first appeared, there have been numerous, almost convulsive, shifts in critical interests, methods, and assumptions. Interest in Perry Miller's kind of intellectual history still lingers, but much modified. Mystical and meditative practices flowered in the 1960s with the appeal of both chemical and spiritual hallucinogens, making what was formerly rare and exotic suddenly everyday. Robert Lowell and others made confessional verse a substantial genre for a time, accompanied by a new and powerful interest in typological biography and autobiography. New Criticism and its attendant Structuralism began their operatic demise, diminuendo and largo. Texts were displaced by readers, readers by semiology and language systems, and everything finally deconstructed to zero at the bone.

These winds of critical interest have not left Taylor unmarked, but they have had little effect upon the main analysis of this study as it first appeared in 1961. Others have shown me that earlier claims for Taylor's personal mysticism were possibly overstated. In this revision I try to emphasize that Taylor could operate within a mystical literary tradition without himself being a mystic. I am now persuaded that the failure to attain mystical assurance was Taylor's main theme (leaving him dependent, therefore, on the vehicle of the church to raise him to salvation). But the mystical framework and tradition still holds as the measure against which he judges himself and others, and therefore is never inappropriate to his poetry. On the issue of the degree to which his *Preparatory Meditations* depended upon and derived from his sermons, I have seen nothing written during the past twenty-five years to dissuade me from my original judgment. There have been no major additions to the biographical information presented here, so that topic remains unchanged in this edition. Otherwise, the energetic and intelligent criticism of the past twenty-five years has not so much challenged or contradicted what I originally wrote as it has added to it or gone off in original directions. In order to make room for an appropriate depiction of this more recent work, much of it of the first importance, I have severely truncated the original treatment of Taylor's earlier and minor poems, particularly the elegies, for which readers should consult the original edition. On the assumption of greater familiarity today with Taylor's verse than could have been presumed a quarter of a century ago, quotations have been severely shortened. The bibliography has been thoroughly revised and updated, but the essential argument remains the same.

Edward Taylor's poetry, his prose, indeed, his entire life were informed by one central purpose, hammered on one anvil, aimed at one end—a blissful eternity in the heavenly city, basking in the radiant vision of Christ, singing His praises and glory. The frontier community near the Connecticut River, pleasant though it must have been at times, was a far cry from the city whose visions dazzled the poet. Yet Taylor saw no impossibility living in the "Suburbs of Glory" even there. His attempt to achieve the glorious life of spirit while still trapped in time accounts for his poetry which is, however, only a part of that attempt. Anticipating the life to come, Taylor could echo Donne's words:

> Since I am comming to that Holy roome,
>   Where, with thy Quire of Saints for evermore,
> I shall be made thy Musique; As I come
>   I tune the Instrument here at the dore,
>   And what I must doe then, thinke here before.

This was Taylor's regular tune, the petition he made constantly: that he, like a musical instrument be attuned to the heavenly harmony; that his spirit, like the string of a lute or a harp, be screwed to the highest pitch, be stretched till it quavered with the angelic choirs. The tension of the image of a soul yoked to a carnal body, yet yearning to fly free of all carnality emblemizes the vital energy behind Taylor's poetry. Unlike Donne, he does not tune his own instrument; instead he prays for Christ to stretch it to heaven.

He might, of course, have relieved the tension by minimizing his worldly attachments, by retiring from the world to a life of pure contemplation. Certainly there is precedent sufficient for this in Christian tradition. But he did not. The social implications of Congregationalism, of Covenant theology, and of the analogy between New Englanders and the Jewish nation provided little room for a recluse. Consequently, Taylor's religious life forced him into the activities of his own community. And these activities of which we have some record stand, like the poems, as parts of Taylor's religious devotion. His marriage and his children; his leadership in the church and his controversies; his preaching and his poetry are all, in a sense, equal acts of devotion. Believing with John Cotton that "not only my spiritual life but even my civil life in this world, all the life I live, is by the faith of the Son of God." Taylor could never, in good conscience, have withdrawn from his worldly involvement any more than he could have expelled his soul prematurely to its heavenly rewards by suicide.

This is not to say that every living act of the man was a *conscious* act of devotion or that his affection for the world was so weaned as to make his activity in it impersonal. Taylor was, on the contrary, deeply involved in the world. But the simple action of setting pen to paper makes a man conscious of his choices and his values, and Taylor was a ready and voluminous writer. Those activities which moved him to write— college assignments; the thrill of a trip across the Atlantic; his love for his wife and his grief at her death; his letters of state and of controversy; and, most eminently, his sermons and poems—were activities he engaged in with full consciousness. It is this life Taylor sometimes describes and sometimes, in a sense, betrays, a life almost uniquely unified in its godliness. And this is the only life of Taylor we really have—that reflected in his own writings.

Perhaps by thus spreading out his devotion, by giving it a wider base in his entire life, by denying as strenuously as he could in his whole behavior the duality of body and spirit, and by making himself personally and socially, in his family, church, and community, the whole creature of God, he somewhat relieved the tension that nearly undid John Donne. Lacking Donne's egocentricity and Herbert's ambition, Taylor was incapable of achieving their dramatic excellence. But more positively, the interrelationship of all the aspects of Taylor's life puts his other activities in peculiar relationship to his poetry. In a way that is true of few other poets, all that Taylor is known to have done comments upon, explains, glosses, accounts for, and provides the motives and the occasions for his poetry. Conversely, to learn what Taylor's poetry is about requires knowing what Taylor was actively about.

For his poetry was not merely an ornament to be included among his social graces but was, like his marriage and his ministry, a duty owed to God.

Norman S. Grabo

The University of Tulsa

Acknowledgments

I must again acknowledge most gratefully the gifted friends and colleagues who critically read this manuscript the first time through— Sam S. Baskett, Meredith Baskett, Clyde Henson, D. Gordon Rohman, and Carrol Joy. An All-University Research Grant from Michigan State University enabled me to prepare the initial study. The Boston Public Library, the Massachusetts Historical Society, and the Yale University Library kindly granted permission to quote from their manuscript collections of Taylor material.

Permission to quote extensively from copyrighted material has generously been granted by the following: American Antiquarian Society for Harold S. Jantz, *The First Century of New England Verse;* Duke University Press for Donald E. Stanford; "The Earliest Poems of Edward Taylor"; E. P. Dutton & Co., Inc., for Evelyn Underhill, *Mysticism;* Oxford University Press for L. C. Martin, editor, *The Works of Henry Vaughan,* Helen Gardner's *John Donne: The Divine Poems,* and H. M. Margoliouth, editor, *Thomas Traherne: Centuries, Poems, and Thanksgivings;* and the Yale University Press for Louis L. Martz, *The Poetry of Meditation* and Donald E. Stanford, editor, *The Poems of Edward Taylor.*

The University of Tulsa has kindly provided the time and encouragement to prepare this revision.

Chronology

1642 Born, probably in Sketchley, Leicestershire, England, at beginning of Puritan dominance; strict Christian upbringing.

1662 Restoration of Charles II; turn of Puritan fortunes; Taylor refuses to subscribe to Act of Uniformity and loses his teaching position at Bagworth, Leicestershire; Half-Way Covenant proposed in New England; Taylor may have attended Cambridge University around this time; writing satirical and occasional poems.

1668 Sails to America; begins diary; his vocation is definitely the ministry by this time; enters Harvard with advanced standing; enjoys friendship of Hull, Mather, Sewall, Chauncy, the prominent leaders of the community; writes several elegies and begins to develop a theory of poetry.

1669 Frontier town of Westfield, Massachusetts, is incorporated.

1671 Commences B. A. from Harvard; reluctantly decides to serve as Westfield's minister.

1673 Westfield urges Taylor to organize the church formally.

1674 Courts in verse and marries Elizabeth Fitch of Norwich, 5 November.

1676 King Philip's War spares Westfield, but the plans to organize the church are again postponed.

1679 Westfield congregation finally enters into a church covenant on 27 August; Taylor is elected pastor and attacks Solomon Stoddard's "liberal" practices in his Foundation Day sermon.

1682 At the age of forty begins his major poetic and devotional activity, the *Preparatory Meditations,* dutifully composed for the next forty-four years.

1689 Wife Elizabeth dies on 7 July; Taylor vents his grief in "A Funeral Poem."

1692   Marries Ruth Wyllys, daughter of a prominent Hartford family; his concern with Stoddard's "apostasy" increases.

1693   Begins series of thirty-six sermons on symbolic interpretation and theory (to end in 1706)—"Upon the Types of the Old Testament."

1694   Attacks Stoddard in eight sermons, A Treatise Concerning the Lord's Supper.

1701   Outlines his Christology to his increasing congregation in fourteen Sacrament-Day sermons, Christographia.

1712   Faction threatens to wreck Westfield; Taylor withholds sacraments to maintain his pastoral authority and defends his action in two sermons on church discipline the following year.

1720   Taylor's fruitful ministry brings him a new and larger meetinghouse; he receives M. A. from Harvard.

1723   Aged and ill, requires temporary assistance of Isaac Stiles.

1725   Writes his last Preparatory Meditation, 8 October; unable to perform his duties, Taylor accepts the help of Nehemiah Bull and assists in his ordination the following year.

1726–1729   Bedridden most of the time after his last sermon from Zechariah 1:5, "Your fathers, where are they? and the prophets, do they live forever?" Westfield adopts Stoddardeanism.

1729   Dies, 24 June; buried in Westfield.

Chapter One
The Active Life

With something of the pride of a spiritual descendant, John Hoyt Lockwood, twentieth-century minister of the church at Westfield, Massachusetts, wrote of Edward Taylor: "It is not an extravagant claim to assert that had he settled in Boston, instead of spending his life on the frontier, he would have been famous in the annals of colonial times."[1] But Taylor did spend his life on the frontier; and, while he remained in high esteem among prominent men of his time, he has been largely ignored by the annalists. In fact, more than two centuries elapsed after Taylor's death before Professor Thomas H. Johnson examined the manuscript book of poetry in the Yale University Library that has now brought Taylor his deserved praise. By publishing some of these poems in 1937, Johnson made the American literary world aware of a long-forgotten, distinguished son.

Professor Johnson was not the first literary scholar to appreciate Taylor's poetic skill—both Thomas Goddard Wright and Josephine Piercy had called attention to it earlier—but he was the first to bring specimens of Taylor's work to light. Taylor's poems established him almost at once and without quibble not only as America's finest colonial poet but also as one of the most striking writers in the whole range of American literature; he had an exceptional quality of mind and spirit for an American Puritan. For in Taylor's poems man is no creature chained by the flesh to a position midway between angels and beasts. Far from being lower than the angels, man comes as close to Godhood as a created nature can; and Taylor boasts that his own nature has been seated in the Trinity. He exults proudly; and he commands even the angels, as a lower order of creation, to "give place" and show him obeisance. "Oh! Admirable," he gloats, "Give place ye holy angels of light, ye sparkling stars of the morning. The brightest glory, the highest seat in the kingdom of glory, the fairest colors in the scutcheon of celestial honor, belong to my nature and not to yours." Even more defiant in verse, he declares without the slightest humility: "I'll claim my right: give place ye angels bright./

I

Ye further from the Godhead stand than I." For the highest honor imaginable has fallen to mankind—God has married man—and this is reason for exultation. Were this notion man's own invention, it would be the grossest blasphemy; but God, not man, makes the claim; and, though the orbs of human reason are dazzled by it, man's only recourse is to accept the God-stated fact.

Like other marriages, this one requires mutual duties; and Taylor does not hesitate to admit that God is dependent upon man as much as he is upon Him. In fact, God needs man. Divine Wisdom has worked out a plan for salvation that permits the loss of no saint whatsoever—a great and enduring source of comfort to those who find signs of God's favor in their own lives. Moreover, the Divine Husband shares His strength with His human bride, communicating to her His truth, grace, life, and wisdom. Hereby man shares God's inmost secrets, knows and participates in the Blessed Life. Again, like earthly marriage, divine wedlock requires consummation; and Taylor sings ecstatic and rapturous songs of love to the Lover of Lovers.

This picture of Taylor, a rara avis singing solitary in the New England wilderness, hardly squares with the common picture of stern Calvinists preaching the depravity of man in a world where moral gloom has overpowered all systematic gaiety. In Taylor there is no stench of sulphur and burning brimstone, no bleak fatalism. Instead his poetry offers honor, pride, sensual and erotic delight, and almost arrogant confidence. Taylor undoubtedly was a rare bird; and, consequently, he has confused critical readers who find him drastically at odds with most evaluations of seventeenth-century Puritanism. Taylor furthered the confusion himself by not publishing any of his writings. A sense of mystery has grown about this injunction—a suggestion that Taylor set pen to paper only "secretly,"[2] and that, therefore, he must have had something to hide. Either Taylor entertained beliefs or attitudes that orthodox New Englanders could neither have sanctioned nor permitted, or the writing of poetry itself was offensive: theologically or temperamentally, he leaned too much toward the rituals and trappings of Roman Catholicism.

But the significant fact is that all historical evidence shows Taylor to have been a very conventional and perfectly orthodox—indeed, conservative to the point of reactionary—Calvinist of the New England school. No full biography of Taylor has yet been written. But the known facts—meager as they seem at first glance—bear out the conventionality of the three major activities of his life: his education, his ministry, and his defense of the New England Way.

Education

Taylor was born in England in 1642, the year in which decades of religious and constitutional agitation finally boiled over into civil war. Parliament had in effect declared itself supreme executive of England; and King Charles I readied for battle in Nottingham, not many miles north of Taylor's home in Sketchley, Leicestershire. Puritans generally joined the parliamentary cause, some even returning from New England where as many as 20,000 religious and political exiles had been erecting a Bible commonwealth for the preceding twelve years. In 1645 the King's forces were defeated decisively at Naseby; and, though Taylor would not have been aware of that event, he was certainly to enjoy its benefits. At least socially and politically there was no stigma to being a Puritan in Taylor's youth.

He retained two especially clear memories of his earliest childhood—the strictness of his parents and his conversion. He seems only to have thought of his parents in terms of discipline. Several times he refers to them together, remembering that their Puritan rigor in no way compromised their Christian love. His childhood habit of lying called forth such sharp reprimands from his mother that in his thirties he could still remember the vividness with which she pictured fire and brimstone. But the single event that impressed him mostly deeply was his own spiritual birth. This occurred early enough in his life for him still to be regularly awakened and catechized by an older sister (there were at least four children in the family). Two mornings in a row his sister recounted stories of the creation and of the life of Christ, and they so impressed him that he dated his real conversion and dedication to Christ from those mornings.[3] From then on he saw his spiritual life as a constant conflict between love, faith, fear, anger, sorrow, joy and hope—a tumult to be controlled only by a well-informed and well-trained reason.

A way to such training and knowledge was open to young Puritans in Taylor's time, but to what extent he took advantage of it is not clear. Certainly, instruction in reading and in Bible history were his at home. And probably he began to study Latin, Greek, and logic quite early. A certain proficiency in languages was required for entrance to the universities, and a long tradition holds that Taylor spent some years at

Cambridge. If he really went to Cambridge, his Latin and Greek would have been necessary for exploring the recesses of scholastic learning. For the universities in England, as on the Continent—and for that matter Harvard—still taught the traditional curriculum of the medieval schools.

Cambridge undergraduates studied three main "arts": logic, which taught correct patterns of thinking; rhetoric, which taught expression according to ancient principles; and ethics, which taught the principles of moral behavior discoverable in the natural world.[4] At Cambridge Taylor may have first absorbed the logical "method" of the educational reformer Peter Ramus—the method later to reveal itself in the construction of Taylor's sermons and in the intellectual structure of much of his poetry.[5] Then, too, the Cambridge system of oral examinations, disputations, and declamations also appears in his American sermons. Taylor might very well, then, have accomplished some of his famous learning in England, but this is not certain. At Harvard the curriculum was so close to Cambridge's that the symptoms of scholastic training in Taylor might have been rooted in either school.[6]

By 1658 Oliver Cromwell was dead, and two years later the fear Taylor must have shared with many another Puritan became a lamentable fact—Charles II was restored to the throne. The years that followed saw one Puritan disappointment after another as Charles reduced the freedoms and privileges of dissenters from the Anglican faith. Taylor felt the pinch of religious intolerance and sovereign displeasure as he never had earlier. Through Charles's Act of Uniformity in 1662, he even lost a position—whether at Cambridge or at Bagworth, Leicestershire, where he reputedly taught for a time, is not clear.

There is no record of Taylor's activities for the next six years. But early in 1668 he made arrangements to try his fortunes in America, and on 26 April he set sail. His little convoy took nearly five weeks to skirt the lower part of England from Gravesend to Land's End. Taylor's impressions of the trip—recorded in a diary—show him equally conscious of three things: the uncertain state of his stomach; unfamiliar birds, fish, and meals; and the necessity of preparing sermons. On 24 May he reports: "I then, being put to exercise, spake from John 3:3."[7] The word "exercise" indicates that Taylor was not a licensed preacher; but the reference establishes the earliest date we have for Taylor's commitment to the ministry. The exercise was not extemporaneous; he indicates in another place in the diary that he worked on his Sunday sermons from at least Thursday.

Appropriately, Taylor first spied New England and the approach to Boston on the fourth of July. Boston, the heart of New England's dream and the center of her commerce, numbered between five and six thousand inhabitants when Edward Taylor walked ashore—it was the largest city in all the English colonies. Settled in 1630 as the beginning of a Puritan Utopia, Boston in 1668 had not enjoyed the warmth of God's smile for some time. Of course there was the college designed to "advance learning and perpetuate it to posterity"; and, though it had recently fallen on hard times, it showed no signs of surrendering its hopes of training a learned clergy. But the early dream had been compromised. The year of Taylor's birth, 1642, had seen a great and troublesome outbreak of sin, and the English Civil War had made New Englanders feel like deserters rather than the vanguard of the Puritan movement. The restoration of Charles II had been a certain sign of God's disapproval, and the compromise of 1662 that threw the doors of church membership halfway open to souls of questionable purity proved again that God's face wore a frown. New England was worried—at least Boston, the conscience of New England, was worried—and its ministers were searching their stores of knowledge, imagination, and ingenuity to find the means of weaning New Englanders from their worldliness, sinfulness, and neglect.

This was the Boston in which the twenty-six-year-old Taylor, armed with several letters of introduction, presented himself to Increase Mather, only three years his senior but already a leading light in Boston's intellectual life. Mather must have welcomed him warmly, for Taylor spent the next two nights at Mather's home. Another letter—to John Hull, Massachusetts Bay's mintmaster and one of New England's wealthiest residents—brought more generous hospitality and flattering attention.

After a week, Taylor went to Cambridge to talk to Charles Chauncy, president of Harvard College. From the seventy-eight-year-old President Chauncy he received both encouragement and an invitation to return in a week. Taylor later spent the night of 22 July in Chauncy's home, and the next morning was admitted to Harvard. Whether making Taylor the college butler and permitting him to take his degree in only three and a quarter years instead of the usual four were acknowledgments of his advanced age and prior education or whether these were inducements to attract another student to a college badly in need of students is not clear. Johnson has attributed Taylor's warm reception to his congeniality,[8] but it may in large part have been due to everybody's recognition that in Taylor stood a potential prop to New England's slipping dream.

Taylor records three experiences from his college days; only one concerns his studies. The first involved Thomas Graves, the senior fellow who tutored Taylor:

> Mr. Graves, not having his name for nought, lost the love of the undergraduates by his too much austerity, whereupon they used to strike a nail above the hall door catch while we were reciting to him, and so nail him in the hall, at which disorder I was troubled. Whereupon, being desired by him to go into the buttery privily and watch who did it, one morning I did so; but being spied by the scholars I was fain to haste out and make haste to Boston before I spake to Mr. Graves, the better to cloak over the business that so the scholars might conclude it was accidental and not *ex propositio* (for I was fearful of incensing them against me). . . . [9]

But Taylor's attempt to cover his duplicity with flight did him little good, for Graves "checked" him when he returned to school. Shortly after this episode Taylor joined his classmates in refusing to study a reputedly inadequate text; the issue forced Graves's withdrawal from the college.

The third incident occurred in the spring of 1670 when Taylor went to pay for his winter's wood. The woodsman's wife, Elizabeth Steadman, accused Taylor of aloofness because he had not visited them more often. Recognizing that "she was a woman of a troubled spirit," Taylor visited her frequently, bringing her "comfort and support." She in turn acted as his nurse when he "was in any kind of affliction," but gossips made him so uncomfortable that by the spring of 1671 he talked to Chauncy about quitting school. The president, still fighting to keep his classes together, persuaded Taylor "by his incessant request and desires" to graduate with his class. In fact, Taylor even planned to return to Harvard that fall as Scholar of the House.

Although Taylor wrote a couple of elegies in his last year at Harvard and delivered a verse declamation in May of that year, no one remarked about his poetic ability. Samuel Sewall, an indefatigable versifier himself, had been induced to go to Harvard by Taylor—they even shared the same bed for two years—and often refers to Taylor in his diary and letter book; but he never says a word about his poetry, which emphasizes Taylor's lack of reputation as a poet. But though his colleagues did not know it—Taylor probably did not know it himself—his Harvard years were training him to be one.

An interest in medicine led him to compile a five-hundred page description of herbs and other medicinals, and this material appeared in his poetry later. Perhaps it was through his acquaintance with John Hull that Taylor first became interested in metallurgy; the interest led him to copy the greater part of John Webster's *Metallographia* (which also found its way into his poetry). The friendship with Increase Mather apparently warmed during Taylor's Harvard years, for Taylor left college an avid follower of all Mather's ecclesiastical teachings. But the college itself was the crowning experience of Taylor's education. It secured his control of Latin, Greek, and Hebrew; it opened for his explorations the tremendous continent of Patristic writings; it grounded him thoroughly in biblical studies and church history; and it honed his abilities against the grating necessity of regular disputations. In short, by the fall of 1671, though he had planned to continue his studies, Taylor was ready for the opportunity that came to him.

Ministry

In 1636 Mr. William Pynchon, seeking to take advantage of a growing trade in beaver furs, founded a settlement on the Connecticut River about one hundred miles west of Boston. Trade was good, and the settlement—called Springfield—so flourished that by 1667 there was room for another trading post nine miles further west. John Holyoke, son of one of the principal settlers, served as minister to the Westfield outpost for a year and then quit. He was succeeded for three years by Moses Hill, but 1671 found the trading post growing into a little farm community and in need of a permanent minister. So in November, 1671, Westfield sent Thomas Dewey to find one.

Dewey first went to Increase Mather in Boston, who sent him with a letter to Taylor. Taylor immediately passed the problem on to President Chauncy and the Fellows of the College. They in turn refused to advise Taylor positively, declaring that they had to consider the good of the college first; this attitude suggests that they thought it to Harvard's advantage to keep Taylor there but did not want to interfere with his job possibilities. Because Chauncy was dead set against the Westfield offer at first, Taylor asked for a week to consider the matter. Taylor's indecision was natural, of course, but in this case it represents a special problem that was to vex him for eight more years. On 18 November, Increase Mather advised Taylor to take the job; and on 27 November, 1671, finding that he had raised Goodman Dewey's expectations so high he could not back out and having secured Chauncy's blessing,

Taylor began "the desperatest journey that ever Connecticut men undertook." Eight days later he arrived in Westfield.

Congregations customarily tested prospective ministers over an extended time. But in 1673 Westfield urged Taylor to continue among them, and his initial indecision returned. He found himself not sufficiently encouraged to organize the church formally; he sensed his intellectual isolation; and he felt he had no roots in the community. Still a student, Taylor purchased what books he could; others he borrowed, making manuscript copies of them for his own library, stitching, gluing, and binding more than a hundred such volumes with his own hands.[10] And when he met with an author's manuscript seeking publication, he willingly wrote to Boston to promote the project.[11] The 192 printed books he managed to collect are impressive for their quality and expense rather than for their number.[12]

But maintaining the intellectual life in the wilderness was not easy. On 29 September 1696, Taylor sent a letter to his college chum Samuel Sewall, now a judge of the Superior Court in Boston. In accepting Sewall's friendly challenge to a debate on the symbolic meaning of the word "Euphrates" in Rev. 9:14, Taylor begins apologetically, saying,

it is so long since I have been engaged in such sort of combats that my weapons are rusty in their scabbards. Yet I have been casting mine eyes into my quiver to find a friendly shaft or two suitable to my poor, simple bowstring. And what I find I entreat you to accept, as heretofore when we were at our pros and cons. I am far off from the Muses' copses, and the foggy damps assaulting my lodgen in these remotest swamps from the Heliconian quarters, where little save clonian rusticity is à la mode, will plead my apology: the mind's arrows are not feathered with silken rhetoric nor piled with academic eloquence.[13]

Perhaps because they recognized Taylor's problem, the townspeople "encouraged" him to stay among them by writing him a formal letter of commendation and by making several attempts to secure David Wilton from Northampton to bolster their struggling church. They hoped that Wilton would encourage their young minister "unto the comfortably carrying on that great work before us, which, when begun in a right way and managed after a right manner, ends in God's glory and our salvation. . . . "[14] Northampton was, however, unwilling to surrender Mr. Wilton; and representatives from Westfield wrote their brethren to the north rather resentfully that "Mr. Taylor is utterly averse to any coalition into a church state without further encouragement, and where to have it, if not from you, we know not."[15] This letter was dated 21 August 1673—the coalition did not come about until six full years later—but within a year Taylor found encouragement from an unexpected source.

How and where Edward Taylor met Elizabeth Fitch we do not know. The first record of their relationship dates from about a year after the rather discouraged letter to Northampton, and it comes in the shape of another letter, this time by Taylor himself and addressed to his "Tender and Only Love." The letter has two parts: the first is a complicated rhymed acrostic in which he promises his heart will be a "ring of love," "Truly confined within the Trinity"; the second is a prose love letter that carefully affirms the relationship of the heart to the Trinity. Human love must be subordinate to the mystical love of the soul and Christ, and Taylor begins the prose part of his billet-doux with the rather blunt "I send you not my heart, for that I hope is sent to heaven long since, and unless it has awfully deceived me, it hath not taken up its lodgings yet in anyone's bosom on this side of the royal city of the Great King. . . ." Yet he assures Elizabeth that she commands all the love he can devote to created beings. Perhaps mockingly, but yet with a sense of seriousness, he falls midway in the letter into a sermon form, arguing the doctrine that "conjugal love ought to exceed all other love"; and after three "proofs," he concludes that "though conjugal love must exceed all other, yet it must be kept within bounds too. For it must be subordinate to God's glory. The wish that mine may be so, it having got you into my heart, doth offer my heart with you in it as a more rich sacrifice unto God through Christ. . . . "[16] Thus did the minister of Westfield work upon another Puritan heart and tie it, as he was later to say, into a true-love's knot with his own.

Elizabeth, too, was afflicted with the Puritan "lust of versification"; on 27 October 1674, Taylor wrote another love poem to her that seems to refer to poems received from her hand: "I had thought that my Muse should have added a quaver or two unto your music, but that stage being so thick a-crowded already, there is scarce any room for it. All therefore that she shall do shall be only to take the tune where you left it and answer, as it were an echo, back again unto your song in this following ditty."[17] The sixty-four line ditty begins with an apology for writing in coarse iambics rather than silken Sapphics, and then proceeds to instruct the bride-to-be in the duties of marriage. In one of his favorite images Taylor develops the conceit of marriage as "That long'd for web of new relation gay, / That must be wove upon our wedden day," a whole cloth decorated with honors, duties, pleasures, faithfulness, and "cares and crosses too." He warns Elizabeth that, if duty, faith, and love are not maintained, the threads of the cloth will snap and the whole web become as irritating and "black as haircloth." Then he concludes:

> It now remains: let's clothe ourselves, my dove,
> With this effulgeant web and our pickt love
> Wrapt up therein, and let's, by walking right,
> Love's brightest mantle make still shine more bright,
> For then its glory shall ascend on high
> The highest One alone to glorify,
> Which rising will let such a glory fall
> Upon our lives that glorify them shall.

Within two weeks they were married.

Thus Taylor sunk roots into the Westfield community, but there was yet another discouragement to keep him from organizing the church. Indian hostilities had threatened for months; and in the spring of 1675, Metacomet, chief of the Wampanoag Indians, united several tribes and led them in a more or less organized series of attacks. Metacomet became known as "King Philip" to the English, and it is by this name that Taylor refers to him in describing the movement of the Indian wars into the Connecticut Valley in the summer of 1675. "Summer coming opened a door unto that desolating war begun by Philip, Sachem of the Pakonoket Indians, by which this handful [at Westfield] was sorely pressed. . . . " By late autumn Westfield was still "sovereignly preserved"; but its preservation was "yet not so as that we should be wholly exempted from the fury of war, for our soil was moistened by the blood of three Springfield men."[18] Through the winter of 1675 and into the spring of 1676, Westfield, now somewhat fortified and garrisoned, suffered occasional raids from what Taylor calls "skulking rascalds," but remarkably escaped a full-scale assault. Agitation to desert the frontier completely had been staved off by Solomon Stoddard at Northampton, who rejected a plan to consolidate the forces of the frontier towns at Hadley and Springfield. Taylor likewise managed to keep Westfield intact, and the spring action really ended King Philip's War for Westfield. Philip's death that year completely concluded the struggle.

The end of the war allowed Taylor to return his attention to the problem of organizing the Westfield congregation into a formal church. Although four of the nine reliable communicants left Westfield with the war, Taylor felt sufficiently encouraged by 1679 to proceed with the ceremonies. Now, thirty-seven years old, with a growing family and eight years of close involvement with the town, he felt firmly rooted there. So in July he circulated letters to several neighboring ministers, requesting their presence. They arrived on 26 August and, in typical New England fashion, immediately objected to Taylor's plans for the following day.

Their most serious objection concerned Taylor's failure to provide a written confession of faith for the congregation. He had intended merely "a professing the doctrine laid down in the *Catechism* of the Assembly of Westminster, so far as it goes, and where it is deficient, to acknowledge the platform of church discipline put forth by the reverend elders and messengers in a Synod held at Cambridge in . . . 1647."[19] But the ministers simply would not accept so casual a confession. The significance of this episode is double: first, it indicates that Taylor's theology and church polity were so conventional he deemed them covered exactly and completely by the Westminster Confession and the Cambridge Platform—more orthodox he could not be; secondly, the ministers, by forcing Taylor to write out the "heads" or principal tenets of his faith, compelled him to reveal the matters of faith he thought most significant. Taylor dutifully entered these doctrines in a manuscript book titled "The Public Records of the Church at Westfield Together with a Brief Account of Our Proceeding in Order to Our Entrance into That State." Nothing Taylor wrote in the following fifty years indicates the slightest modification of these doctrines.[20]

Taylor and six other Westfield men then made "relations" of their qualifications for entering into the church covenant. All seven had arrived at as full assurance as any mortal could that they had been predestined to eternal salvation; that in spite of their heritage of original sin from Adam, Christ had died to redeem them as members of his elect church; that they had experienced special signs of God's saving grace; and that they were, therefore, ready to persevere in God's service. They then signed a brief document called the "Church Covenant," in which they agreed to "give up ourselves unto the only true God in Jesus Christ to walk in his ways with all our hearts" and "to walk together according to the rules of the Gospel in the communion of saints in a particular church instituted state for the carrying on of all gospel ordinances, the ministry of the word, sacraments, and discipline, and also all those mutual duties of helpfulness and subjection in the Lord one unto another. . . . "[21] They then elected Taylor pastor, and were formally welcomed into the family of independent New England congregations.

Taylor's covenant agreements foreshadow his major activities over the next fifty years. Two more wars threatened the frontier during his ministry—King William's War (1690–97) and Queen Anne's War (1701–13)—but while the records note Taylor receiving several pounds of gunpowder or fortifying his house, Westfield never again came quite so close to falling under the brandished tomahawk as it had in 1676.

He preached regularly—usually twice a week—and occasionally displayed his eloquence at Boston.[22] His relationships with his Boston and Cambridge friends remained cordial, and Taylor found himself by inclination and by conviction contributing to Increase Mather's plan to entice people back into active church life by advertising God's illustrious works in New England. This plan, which originated in 1681, resulted in 1684 in Mather's *Essay for the Recording of Illustrious Providences*—a collection of weird occurrences, witchcraft, strange deaths, and even stranger recoveries. Its last chapter is largely the work of Taylor's father-in-law, and Taylor himself sent Mather descriptions of mighty hailstorms, supernatural interventions, and monstrous births.[23] In short, there is no reason to suppose that, had Taylor been closer to the witchcraft activities of 1692, he would have differed at all from the position of Increase and Cotton Mather.

Meanwhile his family cares increased. Elizabeth had presented him with eight children—five of whom died—before her own death in 1689. Three years later Taylor married Ruth Wyllys, and by 1708 had six more children. Throughout this period he filled his commonplace book and his church records with legal opinions about divorce and rape, with admonitions to churches, with advice and inquiries about matters of church discipline, and with a constantly lengthening list of baptisms, marriages, and deaths. By 1703 the meetinghouse had to have galleries built to seat the increasing congregation, and by 1721 an entirely new building was deemed necessary.

But there was one aspect of Taylor's ministry that overshadows all others and has far-reaching implications for the poetry he began composing in earnest by 1682. The main task Taylor set himself and his congregation was to live a life in imitation of Christ. Christ's life, as Taylor constantly reminded the congregation, was a teaching life. Secondly, and somewhat more peculiarly, Christ's life was an artistic life—Christ was the paragon of poets—and in this, too, Taylor sought to imitate him. Over years of study Taylor achieved an exceptional unity of thought in which both views of imitation coalesced; and the result was that his ministry and his poetry became inextricably bound together. Taylor's poetry is what it is because of what he believed and taught as a Christian. For this reason it is important to review his central teaching.

Defending the New England Way

When speaking of the sacrament of the Lord's Supper, Taylor once wrote: "this rich banquet makes me thus a poet."[24] Certainly the sacrament was the occasion for, as well as the subject of, most of his poetry. Also the central concern of his ministry, it naturally occupies a significant position in his preaching.

In part this prominence was a fact of the times that Taylor could hardly have avoided. He had arrived in America only six years after the Synod of 1662 adopted the famous Half-Way Covenant. The Synod urged individual congregations to baptize the infant children of church members, but not to admit them to full membership until they were at least fourteen years old, knew something about the faith they professed, and provided in a public confession or "relation" some evidence that God's saving grace had visited and converted them. The partaking of the Lord's Supper became a lure to struggling half-way members to discover their right to full membership and a public sign of the purest in the congregation. Promoted by prominent churchmen like the Mathers, the practice gained widespread—but by no means total—acceptance in New England. Taylor, whose association with Increase Mather was close, seems never to have deviated from this position. By 1679, the Half-Way Covenant was coming under severe attack, especially from Solomon Stoddard, Taylor's powerful neighbor from Northampton. Taylor was to find that the Christ-like life of teaching meant a life of controversy, and he threw himself into it willingly.

Though Stoddard (1643–1729) and Taylor were nearly the same age, Stoddard graduated from Harvard in 1662, six years before Taylor came to New England, and during Taylor's stay at Harvard was the librarian of the college. While Taylor was finishing his last year at school, Stoddard was being tested by the congregation of Northampton, where he received a call and was ordained in 1672. By that time Taylor was down river in Westfield, looking to Northampton for en-

couragement to organize the church. So far as is known, both men put
into practice the principles of the Half-Way Covenant.

But in 1677, Professor Perry Miller believed, Stoddard began to
baptize "every adult who consented to the articles of faith, and admitted him to the Supper,"[25] thereby giving full support to many who had
been unable to accept the conclusions of the Synod of 1662. It is
questionable that Stoddard had gone quite so far before 1688, but there
is no doubt that he publicized his desire to do so; for in 1677 Increase
Mather, without naming Stoddard, preached to the General Court "A
Discourse Concerning the Danger of Apostasy," attacking Stoddard's
doctrines.

What Stoddard objected to was that, according to the Half-Way
Covenant, no man was permitted to partake of the Lord's Supper until
he had certain knowledge and full assurance of his salvation; without
this knowledge, his attendance at the sacrament was damning. But
Stoddard insisted that no man could know he was saved with absolute
certainty. The only safe course, therefore, was to admit all well-
behaved Christians to the sacrament in hopes that they might thereby
secure saving grace, that they might, in other words, be converted by
it. Since they presumably had not yet experienced conversion, they
need make no "relation" of their religious experience prior to church
membership. Stoddard also argued that the widespread concept of *particular* church covenants was neither scriptural nor necessary; because
God covenanted with a whole people or nation "there is no necessity of
any covenant between the Members of a particular Congregation among
themselves."[26] He concludes that "the supream Ecclesiastical Authority
doth not lye in particular Congregations; if there be no National
Church, then every particular Congregation is absolute and independent, and not responsible to any higher Power: this is too Lordly a
principle, it is too ambitious a thing for every small Congregation to
arrogate such an uncontroulable Power, and to be accountable to none
on earth. . . ."[27] Increase Mather sniffed the dangers in this theory as
early as 1677, and in 1679 his discourse was published.

Of course, 1679 was the year Taylor formally organized the Westfield church. When neighboring ministers arrived that August, Stoddard was among them, having just come from the first of his five
"harvests," revivals demonstrating the efficacy of his policies by the
great number of young people brought to concern for their salvation in
Northampton. He assumed the role of leader at Westfield, as he was to
do throughout the Connecticut Valley; on the following afternoon he

listened to Taylor preach a sturdy Foundation Day sermon that clearly aligned him against Stoddard. Years later Taylor greatly expanded that sermon as "A Particular Church is God's House," categorically dismissing each of Stoddard's arguments and strongly upholding the Half-Way Covenant. But the form Stoddard heard was not provoking, so after the new church members signed their covenant, Stoddard arose and extended his right hand to Taylor with these words: "I do in the Name of the Churches give you the Right hand of Fellowship" (*UW* 1:159). Taylor approved of neither the form of this speech nor its brevity, but Stoddard's civil restraint is one of several instances of his self-control and good sense.

Within two weeks Stoddard had a chance to make his position clear. In Boston to attend the Synod called to deplore the spiritual deadness of the times, he found himself challenged to a debate by Increase Mather. Urian Oakes, then president of Harvard, was to act as moderator. But seeing that wrangling at the Synod itself was not likely to go far to reform the times, Oakes managed to defer the debate until a later time. There is no evidence that Stoddard forced the issue before the meeting on 10 September, which Mather reported in *The Necessity of Reformation* (Boston, 1679). In May of the following year Stoddard had another opportunity when the second meeting of the Reforming Synod gathered to draw up a *Confession of Faith.* The only frontiersman on the committee whose task it was to draft the confession, he again avoided pressing his case.[28]

Meanwhile, Taylor carefully copied his sermon into the "Public Records of the Church" and then made another copy of it to send to Boston. The realization, as Perry Miller puts it, that "there already had been more controversy over the Covenant than the society could stand, and another split over anything fundamental would wreck it,"[29] may have kept it out of print. Or it may simply be that the printer recognized it as a sad piece of writing. In any case, there is no known reaction to Taylor's sermon, and he was content to preserve not only his friendship with Stoddard but peace and amity in the society. By the beginning of 1688, however, he again became alarmed over Stoddard's proselytizing, and he sent him a long letter pointing out that the controversy Stoddard had raised was contrary to the ideal for which New England had been working for over half a century; that his idea was impractical and disturbing to the peace of the church; and—rather prophetically—that future generations would "be ready to date the beginning of New England's apostasy in Mr. Stoddard's motions."

Stoddard answered the letter cordially, but did not attempt to argue with Taylor.[30]

But early in 1694 Taylor, who had worriedly noted Stoddard's growing popularity over the years, preached a series of eight sermons directly against him. These sermons are his longest single treatment of the Lord's Supper; and, therefore, they are most important in respect to his poems. He suggests that sacramental controversies were really what brought the Puritans to America in the first place; for, unwilling to submit to the improper administration of the Supper, "the old and new Nonconformists . . .deserted episcopal governments and suffered persecution, loss of their public ministry, poverty, imprisonment . . . to avoid such mixt administrations of the Lord's Supper; and to enjoy an holy administrating of it to the visibly worthy was that that brought this people from all things near and dear to them in their native country to encounter with the sorrows and difficulties of the wilderness. . . ."[31] To throw over the "thoroughly studied" practice of the founders of New England, as Stoddard was doing, was "grand presumption." Taylor also laments that the "Popish error" of considering the Lord's Supper as a converting ordinance "should bud and blossom among us in New England . . . and yet the same hath been publicly preached to and urged upon the church and people of God at Northampton by the Reverend Mr. Solomon Stoddard the Pastor of the church there" (TCLS, 68). Taylor warns that acceptance of Stoddard's tenets must lead to "downright Arminianism or Pelagianism" (TCLS, 129).

Taylor insists that only the really pure, holy saint may come to the sacrament; for, without the wedding garment of true sanctity, the sacrament is fouled. If, as Stoddard contended, the unsanctified could attend the sacrament merely "to see Christ presented, under the signs, as crucified," this was—to Taylor—reducing the sacrament to a stage show: "as if a man was to go to see a tragedy or stage play; and it doth not answer the case in hand" (TCLS, 123). The sacrament requires the most devout preparation: baptism, hearing the Word, conversion, and "prayer, meditation, and self-examination," which Taylor says "are of special use [to] prepare the soul for this feast." To these he adds contemplation, and so fills out the preparatory requirements for the sacrament.

In describing the preparatory act, Taylor uses the terms "meditation" and "contemplation" interchangeably. Contemplation goes hand in hand with self-examination; they are so close, in fact, that "examination cannot be without contemplation." As a result, he exhorts his congregation to "meditate upon the feast—its causes, its nature, its griefs, its dainties, its reason and ends, and its benefits, etc.—for it carries in its nature and circumstances an umbrage or epitomized draught of the whole grace of the Gospel." Of course this is exactly what Taylor did in his own poetic meditations, which he called *Preparatory*. Such preparation, he adds, will "stir up all sacramental graces: repentance, faith, love, humility, a discerning eye, hunger and thirst after communion with God in Christ, thankfulness, and holy joy in the Lord" (*TCLS*, 198); and these are the very affections expressed in his poetry.

But contemplation is a reward as well as a preparation, for the sacrament strengthens the soul's yearning for union with Christ and sharpens the spiritual eye for a clearer view of Christ:

> Thy contemplations will be raised upon the glory of the wedden, and these will affect thy soul to the glory of God. Think of this. For this will be great benefit. The wedden will set thy contemplations going upon the glory of the wedden, the glory of the king, the glory of the prince the bridesgroom. Oh, the king of glory! How doth it shine forth here? The beauty of the bride, the happiness of the bride, and her honorable preferment. The dowry laid down as his estate to redeem her, to pay her debt, to purchase her freedom, her furniture, her felicity. And that he came to her out of his father's bosom, from his father's palace, on his father's errand, and here in this dirty world was attached to her account, imprisoned, arraigned, condemned, executed, put to death, held a prisoner in the grave till the third day: then he broke the bands of death asunder, threw the prison door off of its hinges, came a valiant conqueror, ascended up into glory, sat at the father's right hand, set up ordinances, sent out suitors his spokesmen, sent down gifts to bestow on his bespoken for, contracts them to him and celebrates the contract now in this wedden feast. So that here you see at the Lord's Supper that contemplation is set awork about these, and that they tend to raise the affections thus, and to bring them to God. *TCLS*, 184–85

And so he describes the Lord's Supper as the highest kind of human activity short of the everlasting life: to belong fully to the church and to partake of the sacrament are to live, he says, in the "suburbs of glory."

Six years after the completion of these sermons, the argument between Stoddard and other advocates of Taylor's position erupted into print. Increase Mather's *The Order of the Gospel*, Cotton Mather's "Defense of Evangelicall Churches," and Stoddard's *The Doctrine of Instituted Churches* were all issued in 1700. But at this time Stoddard and the Mathers have not yet faced-off squarely. Each argues as if unaware of the other's position: Increase Mather defends the Half-Way Covenant as Taylor would have done, and Stoddard positively states his differences for the first time in print. Eight years later, however, with Stoddard's sermon *The Inexcusableness of Neglecting the Worship of God under a Pretence of Being in an unconverted Condition,* the polite fencing ended. Increase Mather attacked "Mr. S" in earnest in *A Dissertation, wherein The Strange Doctrine . . .is Examined and Refuted* (Boston, 1708). The refutation was unfortunately hurried, as Stoddard showed the following year in *An Appeal to the Learned . . . Against the Exceptions of Mr. Increase Mather.*

To come to this debate after reading Taylor's sermons is to court disappointment. For Taylor had exhausted the arguments. Mather lacked either the invention or the time to do a decent job, and Stoddard shames him often with his point-by-point rebuttal. Mather turned to vilifying insinuations; he made it appear that Stoddard was out to deform the church—not reform it—and that his arguments smacked of both treason and Papistry. Stoddard, of course, managed to insinuate the same about Mather and to return the injury in a way that reflects upon Taylor, too. Stoddard declaims: "It seems to me that many Persons do make an idol of the Lord's Supper; crying it up above all Ordinances both of the Old & New Testament, as if it were as peculiar to Saints as heavenly glory. . . . It may be this is some of the relicks of Popish Idolatry, in making the Bread and Wine to be the natural Body & Blood of Christ."[32] He found it easier in this manner to parry Mather than he would have to fend off Taylor, but Taylor's sermons never reached the printer. In 1709 an anonymous pamphlet titled *An Appeal, of Some of the Unlearned, both to the Learned and Unlearned* was published in Boston—a sarcastic retort to Stoddard. The concluding sentences of the pamphlet read: "We hear that Deacon Prince of Sandwich, is preparing an answer to him [Stoddard]. We wish him *good Success;* only we will *Wonder* if he shall convince the Appellant of his *Error,* when all the *Learned Men in the World* have not hitherto been able to do it."[33] Deacon Prince was probably Samuel Prince (1649–1728), or perhaps his son Thomas, who had just received his B. A. from Harvard and was visiting his father in Sandwich in 1709.[34] At some time Taylor's "A Particular Church," the eight 1694 sermons, and a number of other notes in Taylor's hand on Stoddard's notions came into Thomas Prince's possession. Had Prince ever produced the proposed answer to Stoddard, Taylor's influence on American theology might have been considerable; but the book was never written, and Taylor's manuscripts became part of Prince's famous New England Library. These unpublished contributions to the most crucial ecclesiastical controversy of the times prove to be the earliest as well as the most comprehensive refutation of the position called Stoddardean.

Because Taylor based his sacrament-day poems upon his sermons, we know he must have been preaching on the Lord's Supper again from the middle of 1711 through the end of 1712; we have the eleven poems, but not the sermons. At this very time, however, Stoddard was enjoying another harvest at Northampton, and was to have yet one more in 1718. He seems to have made some inroads in Westfield by 1712, for Taylor was having difficulty with his own congregation.

Two sermons in 1713 show Taylor's use of the sacrament as an instrument of pastoral power. In these sermons Taylor defines the minister's authority very much as Winthrop had defined the magistrate's almost a century earlier. He tells the story of a faction that once threatened to wreck the Westfield church until he subdued it by withholding the sacrament not only from the malcontents who opposed him but from all eligible church members. "I knew my office well enough," says Taylor, "and I would not be imposed upon by any."[35] Surely this disciplinary use of the sacrament accounts in part for its eminence in his preaching and poetry.

Taylor's purpose in recalling this unrest to his congregation at the same time of Stoddard's successes in Northampton may well have been to remind them of his knowledge, his power, and his will to keep them to the New England Way. His fight with Stoddard was a long one, and these 1713 sermons may be the first clear sign that it was a losing one.

By 1726 Taylor was quite decrepit, though in that year he attended the ordination of his successor Nehemiah Bull. The very next year Jonathan Edwards went to help his equally aged grandfather at Northampton. By that time Taylor "had become imbecile through extreme old age,"[36] and may not have been aware that in 1728 Bull put before the church at Westfield the following question: "Whether such persons as come into full communion may not be left at their liberty as to the giving the church an account of the work of saving conversion, i.e., whether relations shall not be looked upon as a matter of indifference." A matter of indifference! The church requested six weeks or so to think about the matter, and then "voted in the affirmative"; and it undid in that short span the work of Taylor's entire ministry. On 24 June 1729 Edward Taylor died, and by 1750 only four congregations in the Connecticut Valley still held out against Stoddardeanism; Westfield was not among them.

Chapter Two
The Contemplative Life

A review of Taylor's active life demonstrates beyond question his social and theological orthodoxy, his involvement in the intellectual life of his times, his commitment to all that colonial New England represents. Except for the accidents of place and event that distinguish any individual, Taylor's upbringing, education, and vocation were typical. He was a learned man in an age of many learned men, a frontiersman when the entire continent was still a wilderness, and a man of God in a land swarming with ministers. He detested monarchy, but he played the despot in his own congregation. He denounced Quakers and hated Roman Catholics. He knew there were devils and witches. He believed God exerted His providence in all the minutiae of nature. He thought he was among God's chosen few and that by God's great design the mass of men skidded to everlasting and inescapable damnation. Viewed from the outside, from his "activities"—even his habit of versifying—Edward Taylor was a typical Puritan.

How then is Taylor's obvious unusualness—his peculiar quality of mind, his undeniable artistic accomplishment—to be explained? The kernel of the problem lies in the fact that in our concern for the uniqueness of the New England way, our search for the native grounds of American ideas in Congregational church polity, and our fascination with the intellectual matrix that distinguished the Puritan from his Christian forebears, we have ignored a most crucial side of Puritanism. We have painted our picture in blacks and grays because we at first took the color and light of the Puritan faith for granted—and then forgot about it; and our picture no more squares with the colorful world than a black-and-white photograph does. For the Puritan faith had a gloriously bright side, too; but, in the dark and complicated folds of reform and controversy, we have lost the golden thread of private devotion. Prayer, meditation, and contemplation were as colorfully vivid to the Puritan as to the Catholic, as full of joy, delight, and ecstasy—devotions fundamentally indistinguishable in New England from their practice in medieval Europe and the primitive Christian church. Taylor's best service to his faith may, indeed, lie just in this correction of our view of Puritanism: he casts the color and light of devotional tradition over the historically gloomy face of early New England.

In a sense, Taylor does indeed reflect a Catholic tradition, but he does so with no jeopardy to his own orthodoxy. The boldness of his conceptions, the devotional practice reflected in his writings, the form of his poetry, and even his images and symbols derive unquestionably from the literature of mysticism.

Mysticism begins with the belief or faith that the real nature of the universe is transcendental; reality lies, therefore, beyond the world of phenomena, of sense impressions, and of intellectual abstractions or ideas in the Platonic tradition. The mystic has faith that beyond these is Pure Being, an ultimate spirit or vital principle or energy from which all other forms of being are derived or under which they may be subsumed. Moreover, mysticism contends that men, perhaps especially gifted ones, may, through the discipline of their own spirits, attain a direct experience of this pure being—and not merely a rational conviction of its existence, but a direct and personal acquaintance so complete that it can only be described as a union with ultimate reality. Such a view of reality is ancient and universal, but Christianity has provided a particularly rich proving ground for its development. Its three-personed God, creator of all things, and maintainer of them by His unresting providence, is the Christian's Pure Being, the source of all life and truth, the original and ultimate reality. Omnipresent, and therefore immanent in His creation, He is yet distinct from it to the Christian; He is not pantheistically confused with the nature He has made. The Christian mystic often startles his brethren by claiming that he has attained an intensely close and personal relationship with his transcendent maker—has actually achieved union with God.

The mystic's attempts to describe this ineffable experience, to assure others that the mystical union is really possible, and to urge them to seek to attain it comprise the literature of mysticism. Its documents are strikingly parallel in the process they describe and in the symbols by which they attempt to apprehend the tremendous experience—so parallel, indeed, that they may be called conventions. The mystic process is usually described as an ascension; it begins with curiosity or study of the world and with a growing awareness that the natural world of sense impressions is too transient—too unenduring to answer man's questions

about what and who he is. This recognition which often comes suddenly—like the experience of conversion in traditional Christianity—
often results in contempt for the world. Turning from it, the soul rises to
a transcendent realm, partly by its own mental efforts, but frequently
without any control. This is conventionally described as the soul's being
rapt or snatched to heaven, actually vacating the body for a very brief
time. During this enraptured state, the body becomes senseless and the
person lapses into a trance. The soul, at this time, usually experiences a
sensation of Divine presence and has a vision perceived not by the eyes,
really, but by the mind's eye, the divine spark, or "Funklein," of the
soul. Frequently the soul does not attain union with its "vision" immediately; but, by persistently contemplating this source of all wisdom and
object of all love, it is eventually beatified. The affinity of this experience
with sexual ecstasy accounts oftentimes for the mystic's turning to terms
of sex, love, and marriage to express it. Like Plato's philosopher of the
cave, the mystic does not remain perpetually enraptured; he must de-
scend to a world of shadows and images again. Having viewed ultimate
reality, he desires to communicate his vision to others. His union with
God informs every aspect of his active life.[1]

Awakening

The mystical process is the subject of Taylor's poetry. The first step
in the process—"the awakening of the self" or conversion from the
world of sense—Taylor called "conviction." We must remember that
Taylor subscribed to a complicated and highly refined theology; and its
vocabulary came, in a sense, with his faith and is, therefore, seldom
original with Taylor. Rarely so dramatic as Saint Paul's conversion on
the Damascus road, conviction was yet absolutely necessary in Taylor's
theology. Often very ordinary occurrences occasioned sudden enlightenment: a natural object, a familiar passage from scripture, or the example or exhortation of a well-known friend could unaccountably trigger
the significant experience. Taylor's own conversion occurred in his
childhood; he described it to his congregation on the day of the formal
organization of the first church at Westfield:

As for the first time that ever any beam of this nature did break in upon me
was when I was but small, viz., upon a morning a sister of mine while she was
getting up or getting me up or both, fell on the giving an account of the
creation of the world by God alone and of man especially. . . .

> But oh, this account came in upon me in such a strong way that I am not able to express it, but ever since, I have had the notion of sin and its naughtiness remain and the wrath of God on the account of the same.[2]

This awakening to the sense of the reality of sin, of its dreadfulness, and of his own participation in it betrays Taylor's full realization of an infinite and transcendent God whose will man had crossed. What accounts for his awakening through this rehearsal of a story undoubtedly well-known to Taylor even as a child, Taylor calls the special "work of the spirit of God." He elsewhere considers it a miraculous effect of God's grace. Typically Puritan, Taylor awakens to a conviction of the reality of sin and his own sinfulness as grace affects his conscience. But grace also affects the understanding, according to Taylor, in which case it is called illumination.[3] The two faculties of the soul function together but in opposite directions: conscience struggles to push the soul free from the carnality and worldliness which have led it into sin; and the understanding pulls the soul to the source of light illuminating it, to the personification of wisdom—Jesus Christ.

Taylor's man is above all a rational animal. He cannot legitimately be brought to God without reason. What distinguished man from the other creatures was his rational soul, the link between man and God; and, therefore, God had to be explicable to human reason. Taylor emphasizes this side of his faith even more than most of his colleagues, and they are startling for their rationality. The emphatic point of Taylor's conception of the rational soul is the intellectual faculty—the spark or eye of the soul. Not unique with Taylor, the conception is, however, uncommon among Puritans; it is not so rare among mystics from at least the time of the German Dominican Meister Eckhart (1260?–1327?).

Taylor's God, as I have suggested, is a thoroughly transcendent one; the frequently reprinted "Preface" to *God's Determinations* makes this concept abundantly clear. In it God is maker of the world: turning it on a lathe, blowing the bellows of a mighty furnace, and holding the mold into which the molten Nothing is poured; finally setting it upon pillars, lacing it with rivers and seas, and locking it "Like a quilt ball within a silver box." God's "handiwork" is a very pretty trinket, whose works are under the constant surveillance and control of its Creator's providence. But it remains somehow frivolous: even the glorious sun is reduced to a brilliant bowling ball. Undoubtedly a mighty work, the world glorifies its Maker, but it always remains apart from him. Unlike

Jonathan Edwards's God, Taylor's never becomes so intricately a part of his own creation; for, although Edwards sidesteps the error of pantheism, his expressions walk its very brink. He describes the change in nature that follows an intense experience of God's presence: "The appearance of everything was altered; there seemed to be, as it were, a calm, sweet cast, or appearance of divine glory, in almost every thing. God's excellency, his wisdom, his purity and love, seemed to appear in every thing; in the sun, moon, and stars; in the clouds, and blue sky; in the grass, flowers, trees; in the water, and all nature; which used greatly to fix my mind."[4] Nature never in this way affected Taylor.

The mystic's problem was to find some way of bringing created man to his utterly transcendent God. Unlike the rest of creation, man was made in God's image; Eckhart suggested that this image had nothing to do with man's physiognomy but was a divine nucleus in the soul,[5] which was implanted there to act as a point of contact between man and his Maker. This divine spark seated at the apex of the soul is identified with the highest rational faculty[6] by Eckhart and the German school of mysticism that flowered in the fourteenth century. Taylor, whether aware of their concept or not, echoes the same idea and uses the same image in the last lines of the "Preface." God, having created his glorious trinket the universe, "Gave all to nothing man indeed, . . . / But nothing man did throw down all by sin: / And darkened that lightsome gem in him." Sometimes, as in these lines, the divine nucleus is a gem; at others, a seed, a candle, a coal, or a kernel; but most often it is the spark or eye of the rational soul.

God's grace, like light, shines upon the rational soul and awakens it to the source of all wisdom, Christ. Taylor's Christology emphasizes this aspect of the Savior, fusing him with the classical image of Sophia, or Sapientia, the goddess of wisdom.[7] One entire sermon in Taylor's *Christographia* is devoted to making Christ intellectually and rationally appealing to his congregation. Arguing that since all men desire to attain wisdom and the honor it can bring, he tells them they must "apply themselves in Wisdom's treasury, and trade in Wisdom's markets," which is Christ, in whom wisdom shines "as a clear candle in a golden lanthorn."[8] Of course, Saint Paul had warned against the pursuit of wisdom;[9] but, while Taylor is careful not to go contrary to the Apostle, he seems to have felt with the Englishman Thomas Traherne (1637–74) that "to be a Philosopher a Christian and a Divine, was to be one of the most Illustrious Creatures in the World," and that it was impossible to be truly one without being the others as well.[10]

The beams of Christ's wisdom strike "the intellectual faculty, filling the eye of the soul with a clear sight into all things that are the proper objects thereof" (*C,* 122). This intellectual faculty is the spiritual organ designed especially to receive the "divine light" which Taylor calls "the knowledge of the will of God." "The intellectual faculty is the special seat of this knowledge. This is the eye of the soul whereinto the light of the sun of righteousness is sent and seated. The whole heart is the house into which this sun shines; yet the very cabinet wherein this sparkling pearl which the prophetical office doth hand out is more especially treasured up. The beams of this sun do more especially flutter in this nest, and therein hatch the sanctifying eggs of grace. Oh! Consider this. The sanctifying beams of Christ's prophetical office do gild over the intellectual power with the holy light, whose influences graciously touch the will and affections. . . . The intellectual faculty is the golden candlestick in which the glorious candle of Christ's prophetical chandling is set" (*C,* 371). The highest intellectual organ or faculty is housed in the heart, and the knowledge it brings affects not only the understanding but also the will and affections. Ultimate wisdom and love are inextricably bound together. Taylor declares that there is in human nature a principle for choosing the best; when the intellectual faculty is enlightened, therefore, man must inevitably pursue with all his love and desire that which the intellect has learned to be most valuable.

But not all are graced to see the wisdom that is Christ. Their souls' eyes are, like the "lightsome gem," covered over with sin. Their understandings may occasionally catch some glimpse of Divine Wisdom; but, for full illumination, they require divine and saving light. And this is not given to all: God splits all mankind, exercising what Taylor calls "Selecting Love."[11] The New Covenant or Covenant of Grace, by means of which saving light is distributed, is made only with "the elect of God" (*C,* 372), and not with reprobates who can never attain salvation. Real conviction, when experienced by a person of Taylor's faith, signifies that God is exercising saving grace upon his soul; and therefore proves that that person belongs among God's chosen. The experience of enlightenment or the awakening of the soul, of the illumination of the understanding, and of the conviction of sin—all that marked real conversion—brought assurance and hope of salvation; and such conversion was, indeed, the most reliable sign that God's love had selected him and also the strongest motive for seeking communion with God.

Taylor also was concerned with the soul's awakening at a most mundane level. When God made his "dichotomy" of all mankind, selecting each "name by name," he sent for his chosen "A royal coach whose scarlet canopy / O'er silver pillars, doth expanded lie."[12] The royal coach is the church in which only the sanctified may enter. Some test of the sanctity of those desiring to ride to God's "sumptuous feast" in the royal coach had to be established.

On this question the churches of New England divided in Taylor's time. As to the admission of adults to church membership, liberal practice tended through the last quarter of the seventeenth century more and more strongly to favor admitting all persons of nonscandalous behavior who had a basic knowledge of the principles of Christianity. Many hoped that easy entrance would encourage more people to seek full church membership and thereby, perhaps, reduce the growing sinfulness of New England. But to Taylor and other more conservative ministers, such a course of action was viewed as an abandonment of the principles laid down by the founders of New England Congregationalism, which could only lead the churches to ruin against the rocks of hyprocrisy.[13] Therefore, on the very day he and six other Westfield men gave their own accounts of God's spirit illuminating their understandings and convincing their consciences, Taylor preached a sermon setting out the principles by which the Westfield church was to be run. Revised, the sermon clearly indicated the importance of testifying to the signs of God's special grace awakening the soul: "It is necessary," insisted Taylor, "that the person seeking church fellowship with any church of Christ, give an account of some of his experiences that he hath had of the workings of God's spirit upon his heart . . . (*UW*, 1:299).

Supporting this contention with over twenty pages of argument, Taylor constantly shifts the terms by which he identifies the "matter" or subject of these accounts. Sometimes he calls it a confession of faith, sometimes a confession of sin, a sign of repentance, or a proof of God's "saving work." But essentially it seems that Taylor meant it to be a "confession or relation of some experiences of God's gracious working upon the heart, by the means of grace, holding forth some grounds for Christian charity to judge the old man is put off and the new man put on" (*UW*, 1:299). In his insistence upon admitting only truly sanctified persons, as far as sanctity could be determined, Taylor frequently argued this question of the soul's twofold awakening: the positive illumination that brought faith in Christ, and the negative conviction of sin.

Purgation

Conviction and illumination, working simultaneously, draw forth Taylor's descriptions of the second stage of the mystic way: repentance for sin, disgust at its sight, the attempt to keep the soul's precious eye clear from the foulness of sin, and the denial of carnality and worldliness—in short, the stage of purgation. According to Plotinus, the purpose of purgation is to learn "the meaning of *order* and *limitation* . . . which are qualities belonging to the Divine nature."[14] Underhill says "that which mystical writers mean . . . when they speak of the Way of Purgation, is . . . the slow and painful completion of Conversion. It is the drastic turning of the self from the unreal to the real life. . . . Its business is the getting rid, first of self-love; and secondly of all those foolish interests in which the surface consciousness is steeped."[15] On the one hand, then, purgation involves self-denial and perhaps even self-punishment; on the other, it requires a positive self-discipline and self-formation; on both, it means self-struggle.

The first struggle upon awakening to the signs of God's spirit at work upon the soul is described by Taylor in *God's Determinations* as the soul's exertion to accept the fact that it has been chosen—or as Taylor puts it, "The Elect's Combat in their Conversion."[16] In this poem he pictures the soul as at first bewildered, unbelieving, and resisting God's call in an allegory of war. The soul's resistance arises from its knowledge of its own sin; for, like Michael Wigglesworth's men surprised by the Day of Doom "in their Security," Taylor's elect have been "Lull'd in the lap of sinful nature snug,/ Like pearls in puddles cover'd o'er with mud." Souls completely free from outward sin "are nigh as rare / As black swans that in milkwhite rivers are." Some few immediately give in to the sweet wooing of God's grace, but more commonly their awareness that they do not deserve God's favor sends them in headlong retreat. The second rank of souls surrender to God's Mercy: that is, they accept the argument that, as sinful as they may be, God's mercy is stronger and greater than their own sins; and they yield to God's ability to forgive. The third and last group gives in neither to the first sign of grace nor to the unassisted power of mercy, and it promptly divides into two ranks: the first gives in only when convinced of the justice of election according to God's all-wise plan; the second succumbs only to the combined strength of God's mercy and justice.

But this dramatic allegory of conviction is accomplished very near the beginning of the poem; its greater part is devoted to the accusations of Satan, who represents the convinced conscience, as S. Foster Damon hints rather worriedly. "Satan is the Accuser," Damon says, "and comes perilously near being identified with the conscience. . . ."[17] There is really no peril in this identification. In pointing to the complete unworthiness of the soul to be saved—inwardly and outwardly, even in its worship of God—the conscience functions quite properly; it is satanic in that its accusations purpose to pull the already elected soul away from God, and so run counter to God's will. Taylor is saying that once the soul has evidence of its election, it need not fear the accusations of conscience. Indeed, the Wise and Happy Saint assures the bewildered soul that its doubts are "Satan's temptations," and that the soul must persevere in faith no matter how vicious its conscience claims it to be.

But Taylor does not mean that conscience is absolutely wrong in its condemnation. Like all Puritans, Taylor accepted what Jonathan Edwards was to call "The Great Christian Doctrine": the inheritance of all mankind, and indeed one of its defining characteristics, is the defect of sin—the doctrine of original sin. Calvin writes that man as a whole is in every way defective; he is, in a sense, the blotch and defect of nature itself: "man is of himself nothing else but concupiscence." Carefully defining the term as he finds it used by Paul and Augustine, Calvin asserts: "Original sin, therefore, appears to be an hereditary pravity and corruption of our nature, diffused through all the parts of the soul, rendering us obnoxious to the Divine wrath, and producing in us those works which the Scripture calls 'works of the flesh.' "[18] Not the work of nature but the proud disobedience of man himself in the person of Adam is responsible for our defect, he insists. Calvin isn't concerned with how this sin is transmitted; the important thing is to accept the fact that Adam's sin is inherited. "Nor," he says, "to enable us to understand this subject, have we any need to enter on that tedious dispute, with which the fathers were not a little perplexed, whether the soul of a son proceeds by derivation or transmission from the soul of the father, because the soul is the principal seat of the pollution."[19]

But the transmission of original sin—exactly the kind of question that fascinated a mind like Taylor's—received his attention as he preached about purification in 1701. What would have to be done, he asked, to permit a pure and undefiled human nature to come into being? Human nature, according to his considerations at that time, was composed of two essential parts: (1) the physical materials, and (2) the rational soul. No creature can be sinful unless it is rational; but the rational soul is, for each individual, made immediately ex nihilo, of no preexisting matter, and therefore is in itself pure. As soon as it is infused into the physical materials, however, the combination becomes sinful. But neither are the physical materials, before this infusion, sinful in themselves; they are merely what Taylor calls "fallen nature." Though not properly sinful, this fallen nature requires purification because it is the part inherited from Adam. What identifies it as fallen or defective is its "inclination to any vice, or sensual motion disordinate. . . . There is in the spermatic principals, the original of all indisposition unto, and opposition against, all sanctity and righteousness, as a consequent of the loss of God's image in holiness, by sin . . . which, when the rational soul is infused, making it perfect human nature, then this original of these things is indeed original sin inherent; and this is found in all conceptions made in an ordinary way." Of course, since Adam, only one human nature had come into existence purified prior to being infused with a rational soul: the extraordinarily purified human nature of Christ.[20]

All others faced the impossible task of purifying a nature already thoroughly sinful. Taylor's personal offenses, confessed in his "relation" to the Westfield church, seem singularly unworthy of the great work they illustrated. And Taylor himself admitted that "being under the rigid and watchful eyes of my parents who would crop the budding forth of original sin into any visible sins with wholesome reproofs, or the rod, I was thereby preserved from a sinful life. But yet the transgression of the Sabbath and some degree of disobedience to my parents, and too often the evil of lying and also inward evil were things that did more prevail, all which have had their oppositions by one reproof or until they have been a burden unto me." (*UW,* 1:99). The founders—"foundation men," or "pillars"—of the church were never chosen easily in New England; for public confessions of "innocency of life" were viewed by partial and impartial neighbors alike with sharp and not always charitable criticism.[21] Yet no one seems to have questioned the mildness of Taylor's confession.

Moreover, Taylor provides two strong reasons for supposing that had there been more to confess to, he would have made it public. First, of course, the blacker the sin, the more powerfully God's spirit could be seen to have worked in the repentant sinner; and, therefore, the better and more encouraging an example he would be for others in the gathering. And secondly, the strength of the church grew from the mutual dependence of its members. One way to secure that strength was to submit to the charitable love of others in the church by throwing oneself upon their loving forgiveness. Presumably the more self-degrading the spectacle was and the more love required to forgive, the more intimate one's reliance on fellow church members became, and the stronger became the church itself (*UW*, 1:339–41). But apparently Taylor could muster no such visible sins.

Invisible sins, however, were another matter—if we may judge from his *Preparatory Meditations,* the poems written at regular intervals from 1682 to 1725. The very first confesses to a "streight'ned breast," a "lifeless spark," and a cold love; and late in 1722 he still complains that his soul is diseased, too barren a ground for him to expect Christ to be implanted there. In fact, his poetry, in which he never mitigates the foulness of his sins by euphemistic language, creates a picture of his sinfulness in startling contrast to his public confession. "Filth" recurs frequently throughout the meditations, and Taylor is rich in figures of speech to vivify the word: he calls himself a dirt ball, a muddy sewer, a tumbrel of dung, a dung-hill, a dot of dung, a varnished pot of putrid excrements, drops in a closestool pan, guts, garbage, and rottenness. He wears a crown of filth, his cheeks are covered with spiders' vomit, and he is candied over with leprosy. He is also a pouch of passion, a lump of loathsomeness, a bag of blotches, a lump of lewdness; and he gives off a nauseous stink. He is wrapped in slime; pickled in gall; a sink of nastiness; and a dirty, smelly dish cloth: he is, in short, "all blot."

Much of Taylor's language is conventional, and certainly his attitude is. But the images bark too energetically to be discounted as mere shams or conventions; Taylor very really felt himself to be sinful; in fact, to be utterly helpless against his sins. He allegorizes in military terms the struggle in his own soul in *God's Determinations.* The thousand griefs that one faces in life violate integrity, forcing surrender to sin itself; as soldiers of sin, they

> march in rank and file, proceed to make
> A battery, and the fort of life to take.
> Which when the sentinels did spy, the heart
> Did beat alarum up in every part.

We should notice that, while it is the heart that becomes the last stronghold against sin, the heart is not the symbol of emotions in our common use of the word: it is the proper seat of knowledge, which houses the divine spark, the intellectual faculty. Sin penetrates most deeply in the form of "peeping thought, sent scout of sin" (*PM*, 2.42), so the struggle against sin becomes an intellectual combat in the heart. "For the battle must be fought where the enemy is quarter'd, and that is in the heart. You see, they are enemies in the mind. So the carnal mind is enmity. . . . Now then the enemies to be slain are the inhabitants of the heart. The rebels are quarter'd there" (*C*, 60).

The thoughts most injurious to the clear sight of the eye of the soul are those of the "carnal mind," the attraction to things of this world. "I'm but a flesh and blood bag," he complains: "Passion, pride, lust, worldliness, and such like bubs . . . bow my heart aside" (*PM*, 1.43). He finds his love hugging the brambles grown around his heart rather than his Lord. His heart is too small, "Tartariz'd with worldly dregs dri'd in 't." Knowing his heart should be turned to God, he sees it nonetheless "run out to / Poor bits of clay: or dirty gays embrace" (*PM*, 2.11). Thus his conscience interminably accuses him; Satan tells the convicted soul that its worldliness, like all its vices, are natural to it, "For sins keep sentinel within thy heart" (*Poems*, 424). Humiliated to the edge of despair, Taylor cries out, "Unclean, unclean: my Lord, undone, all vile / Yea for all defil'd: What shall thy servant do?" (*PM*, 2.26).

The work of ridding his heart of its worldliness cannot be carried on but by "the heart searcher, and this is God alone" (*C*, 61). It is He who must "Scour these quarters," gibbet up "each peeping thought" of the world, and "quarter here each flourishing grace." Because Taylor finds the source of his sins not merely in his passions or will but in the very root of his being, he is incapable of removing them by his own exertions. Only Christ can purify him.

Taylor insists so much upon ceremonial cleanness in talking about the church that one would expect him to emphasize the Old Testament rite of circumcision. But he concerns himself with it very little; in Meditation 2.70 (1706) he considers circumcision most directly: there is no question but that man must undergo the knife to cure his soul of sin and "proud naughtiness":

> The infant male must lose its foreskin first,
>   Before God's Spirit works as pulse, therein
> To sanctify it from the sin in't nurst,
>   And make't in grace's covenant to spring.

Must there be actual cutting then? Taylor says "No, no. Baptism is a better mark. / It's therefore circumcision's rightful heir / Bearing what circumcision in't did bear." Circumcision, therefore, a part of the Mosaic Law, is merely a symbol or "type" of the New Testament's baptism, which ceremonially purifies the newborn soul after conversion. Its symbol changes from a "keen and cutting sharp" one to one of washing. As important as this sacrament is, however, Taylor says very little about it directly in either poetry or prose. Circumstances, as well as his own interests, turned his attention from the initiatory seal of baptism to the confirming seal of communion.

But this turn of attention in no way limits the variety of purification images. Arrows and swords of God's righteousness play an active part, but purification comes much more frequently through washing or scouring. Christ is a spring or a well, a pool or a cleansing shower, a laver, or fountain of aqua vitae, whose blood scours the soul of all sin. Most often, however, the purification is by fire; and in repeated images, Christ is the sun whose hot rays melt the frozen lake of Taylor's affections, disperse the black clouds of sin, or enlighten the eye blinded by it. Sometimes He is a spark falling into Taylor's tinderbox of sin; at others, a flame dropped into the poet's hearth, burning up the trash of worldliness; or again, a furnace in which Taylor's heart is melted like ore. Purification is compared to the refining of gold from the dross of sin and worldliness. Taylor pleads repeatedly for a coal from God's altar to be placed on his tongue, or for himself to be made a sanctified altar upon which to offer his own heart as a sacrifice. Often his heart itself is a coal covered with ashes that must be blown clear before the fire of love can burn, or it is a candle that must burn sin's fat to remain lighted.

In another set of related figures, purgation is a grinding process, or his heart is hammered into a godly frame on the anvil of Christ's authority. He begs to be made the valley in which the Lily Christ is planted; but he must consequently be prepared by tearing, plowing, and harrowing—thus the dung of sin is made the fertilizer for sweet graces (*PM*, 2.84). From the purified field come the sweet graces and herbs, medicinals in the hands of the Physician of physicians. Purgation is always left to Christ in Taylor's writing; for, although one can will to be pure, the doing remains with Christ. "Without a miracle there is no cure," writes Taylor, and so the Sun of Righteousness becomes a "surgeon's shop" where Taylor presents his sinful soul for cleansing.

In this negative aspect of purgation, Taylor often seems to approach traditional asceticism; but his self-punishment never reached the extremes of mortification reflected in Catholic hagiography. The "loathsome ordeals" described by Underhill in the lives of Saint Francis of Assisi, Saint Catherine of Genoa, Madame Guyon, Saint Ignatius Loyola, and other mystics[22] appear neither in the writings nor in the life of Taylor. But because Taylor did not put stones in his shoes or wear chains next to his body or seek out ugly sores to kiss, he is not to be disqualified from the spiritual life. Perhaps to a man as highly sensitive to words the verbal whiplash provides as effective self-flagellation as a physical whip could.

Abundant as the evidence is for the darker side of the purgative way in Taylor, proof of a more positive self-discipline and self-formation also abounds. It comes not from Taylor's poems, however, but from his sermons, especially the *Christographia* sermons preached from 1701 to 1703. Actually a unified study of the nature, properties, and operations of the Redeemer, the fourteen sermons commonly sound one distinctive note: the necessity of imitating Christ. Taylor tells his congregation that it is one thing—and a very necessary thing—to worship and praise God with the mouth, "But this honor without the heart is but a vain shew"; and so he urges his congregation: "Strive to hold forth the glory of the person of Christ in your Christian life and conversation." In almost every exhortation he returns to this duty. It being God's plan to redeem fallen man through divine mediation, He, in the person of Christ, took on a human nature. For this gift, we ought "to live more to the honor of God, than the angels themselves in that our nature is more honored" (*C*, 32). Our will and judgment being under the cloud of original sin, our surest way to a virtuous life is through the imitation of the most Godly of men.

In fact, we imitate by nature, instinctively: "We were made and formed with an imitating principle in our nature, which cannot be suffocated or stifled, but will act in imitating some example. God, to prevent us from taking wrong patterns to follow, hath presented us with a perfect pattern of right practice in our own nature in Christ, which is most exemplary, being a most exact copy, written by the son of God with the pen of the humanity on the milk white sheet of an holy life. Hence our imitation of him is his due and our duty, and to leave this pattern is to dishonour him, deform our lives, to deviate from our pattern, and to disgrace ourselves" (*C*, 34). For this reason, Taylor's task in the *Christographia* is to write an extended character sketch of the perfect model and to encourage his congregation to follow it.

What Taylor pursues in the *Christographia* is not a dramatic character-
ization like *God's Determinations* but a profoundly analytic study of the
character of Christ; it is rational rather than emotional, representing
that traditional stage of mystic development that often accompanied
"the Purification of the Self"—the process of recollection or meditation.[23] In Taylor's mind, meditation and faith go hand in hand, though
he employs a rather more bovine image. Meditating on Cant. 6:6, "Thy
teeth are like a flock of sheep that come up from washing whereof every
one bears twins," Taylor writes:

> This faith and meditation a pair appears
>   As two like to the two brave rows of teeth
> The upper and the nether, well set, clear,
>   Exactly meet to chew the food, belief.
>   Both eat by biting: meditation
>   By chewing spiritually the cud thereon.

"Christ's milk white righteousness and splendent grace"—the perfect
pattern to imitate—become the particular food to be chewed by
meditation.

From the beginning of the sixteenth century there appeared on the
Continent and in England an increasing number of guides to the spiritual
life—to prayer, contemplation, and devotion generally. Emphatically
they urged the duty of prayer, both public and private; and they gradu-
ally identified private prayer with meditation, which they treated sometimes as self-examination, sometimes as secret or closet prayer; but they
made it a necessary action of the devout life. Progressively they came to
define meditation, distinguishing it subtly from other very similar acts
of devotion. Until the beginning of the seventeenth century, the most
prominent of these works were written by Catholics and were brought to
England largely through the proselytizing of the Jesuits.

Quite naturally, then, Professor Martz, in his fine study of *The Poetry
of Meditation* (New Haven: Yale University Press, 1954), turns to Richard Gibbons of the Society of Jesus for a contemporary definition of
meditation. Gibbons succinctly defines it as thought "deliberately directed toward the development of . . . 'love and exercise of vertue, and
the hatred and avoiding of sinne.' " Saint Francis de Sales modifies this
definition somewhat by distinguishing the exact mode of thought:
". . . when we thinke of heavenly things, not to learne but to love
them, that is called to meditate: and the exercise thereof Meditation."[24]

Love, not knowledge alone, is the end of meditation; and the peculiar relation between love and knowledge is its distinctive feature. Underhill comments that "there is a sense in which it may be said, that the desire of knowledge is a part of the desire of perfect love: since one aspect of that all inclusive passion is clearly a longing to know, in the deepest, fullest sense, the thing adored. . . . But there is no sense in which it can be said that the desire of love is merely a part of the desire of perfect knowledge: for that strictly intellectual ambition includes no adoration, no self-spending, no reciprocity of feeling between Knower and Known. Mere knowledge, taken alone, is a matter of receiving, not of acting: of eyes, not wings: a dead alive business at the best."[25] Gaining knowledge, not for its own sake, but for the sake of love, "comes to be regarded," writes Martz about the first half of the seventeenth century, "as an exercise essential for the ordinary conduct of 'good life' and almost indispensable as preparation for the achievement of the highest mystical experience."[26]

While Taylor describes the act as a chewing of the cud, others also emphasized its nature as an exercise. The most exacting and detailed of these descriptions is probably Saint Ignatius Loyola's *Spiritual Exercises,* which details a series of ordered and predictable but not utterly inflexible stages. First the "exercitant"—as Loyola calls one who meditates—attempts to fix his attention on some "heavenly thing" such as some scriptural incident or venerated object in order to secure as lively an apprehension of it as he can by an effort of memory and imagination. Then he submits the object of his contemplation to a lengthy, rigorous, and thorough intellectual examination until his understanding of it is complete. The next step is to judge or evaluate the object, after which the exercitant submits his evaluation to his will and affections, which are moved according to the attractive excellence or repulsive sinfulness of the object. The final stage expresses these moved affections—usually joy, love, praise, gratitude, or sorrow—in a colloquy with the Lord. Loyola's directions, in one form or another, gained wide distribution in England; and they exerted, with De Sales's *Introduction to the Devout Life* and Lorenzo Scupoli's *The Spiritual Combat,* a considerable influence upon the devotional practice of English writers, notably upon Donne, Herbert, Crashaw, and Traherne; they also created a demand for similar books by non-Catholics.

In 1648 the popular *Shorter Catechism* of the Westminster Assembly—the statement of doctrine about which Puritans of Old and New England agreed, and which Taylor in 1679 wanted to make the primary basis of the Westfield church's statement of faith[27]—made the practice of meditation a clear duty in approaching the sacrament of the Lord's Supper; and a year later Puritans had their own handbook of meditation in Richard Baxter's *The Saints Everlasting Rest*. The fourth part of this book, "one of the most popular Puritan books of the entire seventeenth century,"[28] expounds at greater length and in greater detail than any other English book what Baxter calls "this Art of Heavenly-Mindedness." He titles this section "a Directory for the getting and keeping of the heart in Heaven: by the diligent practice of that Excellent unknown Duty of Heavenly Meditation."

In defining meditation, Baxter echoes De Sales's emphasis on love. Too often Christians "have thought that Meditation is nothing but the bare thinking on Truths, and the rolling of them in the Understanding and Memory! when every School-Boy can do this, or persons that hate the things which they think on."[29] Baxter's strength lies not only in the vigor of his expression, but in the boldness with which he calls upon the rich Catholic tradition of mystical literature. His marginal gloss ranges widely, once citing Jean Gerson's *De Monte Contemplationes* with the surprising advice: "Read this you Libertines, and learn better the way of Devotion from a Papist!"[30]

His meditative method itself, like Loyola's, follows the exercise of the various faculties of the soul. First the understanding "must take in Truths" and store them in its "Magazine or Treasury"—the memory. Bringing these truths from the memory to the affections requires "Ratiocination, reasoning the case with your selves, Discourse of minde, Cogitation or Thinking, or, if you will, call it Consideration."[31] This is also Taylor's understanding of meditation; like Baxter, he sees this intellectual analysis preceding the act of love itself but tending always to produce it. "Impower my powers, sweet Lord," he petitions, "till up they raise / My 'fections that thy glory on them blaze." For Baxter makes the rational discipline the necessary bridge between the head and heart, over which the truths of the understanding must pass to be judged good or bad by the will, and then submitted to the affections, usually love and joy.

Taylor knew Baxter's work, as did most thinking New Englanders of his day; consequently, it is not surprising to see one of Baxter's ideas affirmed in Taylor's practice. Baxter sees this positive aspect of purgation closely related to the negative one—as closely involved, in other words, with the struggle against sin. He urges meditation as a duty, even when the spirit is dry and unresponsive. "I know," he says, "so far as you are spiritual, you need not all this striving and violence; but that is but in part, and in part you are carnal; and as long as it is so there is no talk of ease."[32] The exercise must be performed, willingly or not, until the heart achieves the joyful rewards it seeks. Verbalized, this self-struggle takes the form of a soliloquy, which Baxter describes as "a Preaching to ones self."[33] Martz writes that "a curious and typical Puritan twist" then occurs when Baxter says that "Therefore the very same *Method* which a *Minister* should use in his preaching to others, should a Christian use in speaking to himself." Actually the twist is neither so curious nor so typically Puritan as Martz suggests since similar injunctions recur commonly in sixteenth-century devotional guides.[34] But the injunction was singularly appropriate to Puritans, whose "method" in preaching was quite distinctive; and to Taylor in particular, whose preaching conforms essentially to Baxter's meditative discourse of mind.

Echoes of Baxter's *Saints Everlasting Rest* resound through the pages of American devotional guides, especially those written by Increase and Cotton Mather and their colleague Samuel Willard, whose works appear in Taylor's library. Evidence indicates that Taylor's practice of meditation dates from at least the time of his emigration to America, but it is nonetheless appropriate that Increase Mather's *Practical Truths* should have declared the nature and aim of meditation as Taylor observed it the very year Taylor's *Preparatory Meditations* began.

Mather's eight sermons of *Practical Truths* comment on the duty of public and private prayer; and he identifies meditation with the latter in a consideration of the practice of Isaac (Gen. 18:23), of whom it is said: "*That he went out to meditate;* or (as the *Hebrew* word . . . may be read,) *to pray.* The word signifieth both to pray and to meditate, and it is not improbable but that *Isaac* did at that time nothing but what was his daily custom to do, even retire himself from all company, for secret prayer and meditation."[35] Mather describes the aim of such secret prayer, as he frequently refers to it, as a mystical "intimacy of Communion with God"; its method is primarily a careful "particular" examination of conscience, the logical divisions of which correspond to the number of sins in question; and its effect is to stir the affections to "*a godly sorrow* for sin." But with this conviction of sin there also comes a "hungering after Christ. The soul must stand affected towards Christ as a hungry man doth towards food." Of course the Lord's Supper is the only feast at which Mather imagines that this "hungering after Christ" can be satisfied.[36] With this concept, he follows the long line of Catholic and English writers who felt the connection between meditation and the sacrament of communion to be necessary and inevitable.

In this attitude, Mather anticipates Taylor's own concern for meditation, which he addresses as part of preparing to receive the sacrament. Preaching about the necessity of approaching the sacrament in a pure state, Taylor urged his congregation in 1694 to "Carry a sacramental frame along with thee. Stir up all sacramental graces; repentance, faith, love, humility, a discerning eye, hunger and thirst after communion with God in Christ" (*TCLS,* 198). In agreement ideally as well as verbally with Increase Mather, Taylor insists first upon cleanliness from sin: "Stand clear from sin. . . . O! abhor it, come not nigh it: fly from it; both in heart and life purge away this evil thing, both in heart, affections, and conversation." Moreover, he urges what must sum up his idea of imitating Christ as he continues: "Be much in the exercise of love, patience, meekness, faith, hope, joy in the Lord, repentance, self denial, prayer, meditation, and the like" (*TCLS,* 199). And finally, like Mather, Taylor closely identifies meditation with the examination of conscience.

Taylor would have the examination of conscience be two-fold: first, of the worthiness of the soul, which includes a review of one's conviction and conversion; and secondly, of the merit of the person outwardly in one's visible holiness, personal reformation, and knowledge of the spiritual mystery of the sacrament. But examination itself can only be part of the preparation. "Examination cannot be without contemplation," says Taylor; and he therefore urges his congregation to meditate as well. In this directive he clearly reflects his own meditative concerns, and he appears to be urging others to follow his own example: "Meditate upon the feast, its causes, its nature, its guests, its dainties, its reason and ends, and its benefits, etc. For it carries in its nature the circumstances as umbrage, or epitomized draught of the whole grace of the Gospel. For our Saviour is set out in lively colors" (*TCLS,* 203). These are also the major subjects of his own sermons—those he thought most worthy of preserving.

In greater detail Taylor presented the considerations proper to a full meditation of Christ in the sacrament. We should meditate upon "Our utter and eternal ruin by sin" and upon Christ's death for it; the covenants of redemption and grace; and Christ's role in the covenants, including his assumption of human nature, his fulfilling of the law in his human nature, and the application of this action to the elect (*TCLS,*

203). This catalogue describes almost exactly what Taylor presents in the *Christographia* sermons: a detailed picture of Christ, designed to show his excellence and loveliness by a dry and intellectual analysis of "Christ's Person, Natures, the Personal Union of the Natures, Qualifications, and Operations."[37]

The ratiocination called for by Richard Baxter—and, indeed, the initial acts of the memory, understanding, and reason that Loyola and most others made the rational cud-chewing part of the meditation— Taylor practiced himself as he pondered his sermon material and reduced it to method. His analysis yielded a full realization of Christ's excellence, which he in turn praised in song. That song, addressed to Christ and called a "Preparatory Meditation" by Taylor, is not really complete in itself; but it marks what Loyola called the last stage of the formal meditation—the "colloquy with the Lord." Thus to be fully understood, the poem must be read with its accompanying sermon in which the intellectual analysis is carried out rigorously, in which the food of belief is chewed most finely between the grinders of faith and meditation.

Rapture

Soon after the soul on its mystical quest awakens to the desirability of Christ, purges itself of carnality and sin, and militantly undertakes to discipline itself in virtues and through the mental exercise of meditation, it is frequently rewarded by visions, voices, and ecstatic raptures. Underhill describes these as encouragement to the novice to continue the mystic quest. Both she and Dean Inge insist that such "mystical phenomena" belong only to the beginning stages of the "unitive way,"[38] and recent students of the subject join both in making such experiences purely extrinsic, as quite unnecessary to the mystical experience.[39]

But when Inge adds that "Self-induced visions inflate us with pride, and do irreparable injury to health of mind and body,"[40] he does an injustice to the seventeenth-century practice of meditation. Taylor's meditations—the exercise of the rational faculties applied analytically to the nature of the Mediator—were designed especially to induce an exceptionally clear image of Christ's excellence and loveliness or, in effect, a vision. The difficulty of treating this subject of visions in the mystical process is complicated by the fact that we are studying a sensitive artist's expression. For example, Vaughan writes:

> I saw ETERNITY the other night
> Like a great *Ring* of pure and endless light,
>   All calm, as it was bright,
> And round beneath it, Time in hours, days, years
>   Driv'n by the spheres
> Like a vast shadow mov'd.[41]

Are we to take this as descriptive of an actual, though hallucinatory experience, or is it purely imagined symbol, a visual metaphor designed to give concrete vividness to a difficult abstraction? Was there a ring of light that Vaughan saw either with his eyes or in his imagination, or does he create the ring himself to embody in it his "sense" of eternity? The same questions occur in the study of Taylor.

The purpose of his meditations was to produce a vision, not perhaps for his physical eyes, but for the eye of the soul that is the mirror or image of God in him. In highly conventional mystical language, Taylor expresses his desire to achieve a vision of the Lord in 1715: "Lead me, my Lord, upon Mount Lebanon, / And shew me there an aspect bright of thee" (*PM*, 2.125). Once the divine spark of the soul is conceived to be an eye, visual imagery follows both naturally and appropriately; and it is difficult for this reason to be sure that Taylor describes an actual experience. What the soul's eye sees, of course, is Christ's incomparable beauty, which prompts the soul to desire Him. Taylor's frequent use of terms like *ecstasy, enravishment, rapture,* and *rapt* invites us to reason that he experienced heavenly visions quite often. But he seems to claim actual visions on very few occasions. One he describes very consciously as a daydream or a vision in the imagination. But Taylor does seem to suggest that it actually occurred:

> My shattered phancy stole away from me,
>   (Wits run a wooling over Eden's park)
> And in God's garden saw a golden tree,
>   Whose heart was all divine, and gold its bark.
>   Whose glorious limbs and fruitful branches strong
>   With saints and angels bright are richly hung.
>
> (*PM*, 1.29)

Taylor identifies the tree as "The tree of life within God's Paradise," compared to which he finds himself "a withred twig." The remainder of the poem is devoted to an explanation "with careful analysis, [of] the exact relation of Man to God by developing the central image of a 'Grafft' upon that tree."[42] But the tree returns again as the central image of a "vision" in the second series of Meditations. Again the poet imagines himself in "Eden's park":

> Walking, my Lord, within thy Paradise,
>   I find a fruit whose beauty smites mine eye
> And tastes my tooth that had no core nor vice.
>   And honey sweet, that's never rotting, lie
>   Under a tree, which viewed, I knew to be
>   The tree of life whose bulk's Theanthropie.
>
> And looking up, I saw its boughs all bow
>   With clusters of this fruit that it doth bring,
> Nam'd greatest LOVE.
>
> <div align="right">(<i>PM,</i> 2.33)</div>

But from this point on there is no sense of actually seeing a tree, and Taylor attends in the rest of the poem to the implications of what he has seen.

Very early in the first series of meditations, however, Taylor alludes most clearly and significantly to a not uncommon visionary experience among mystics.[43] He describes this in "The Reflexion":

> Once at thy feast, I saw thee pearl-like stand
>   'Tween heaven, and earth, where heaven's bright glory all
> In streams fell on thee, as a floodgate, and,
>   Like sunbeams through thee on the world to fall.
>   Oh! sugar sweet then! my dear sweet Lord, I see
>   Saints' heavens-lost happiness restor'd by thee.

That this vision, which Taylor treats so matter-of-factly, should have occurred at the sacrament ("thy feast") is highly significant of the intense concentration Taylor brought to the Lord's Supper. But he does not treat the vision as an exceptional experience in its own right; for in the next stanza of "The Reflexion" he drops the floodgate vision and returns to the central image of the poem—Christ as the Rose-of-Sharon. This indicates that his "visions" are less actual than imaginary, and this interpretation seems valid since Loyola and Baxter and other guides to the spiritual life encourage the use of imagination to vivify the matter of their meditation. But visions and preternatural experiences aside, Taylor seeks, both as mystic and communicant, complete loss of his own identity in God, union with his Maker.

Union

Taylor's conception of this mystical union with the divine is perhaps the most significant in his writing. He discusses union in several ways: the "hypostatic" personal union in Christ, the mystical union between Christ and his church, the natural union of Christ with his human kinsmen, and the sacramental union which signifies all three. These are mutually related, but it is useful to consider them separately.

In the theology espoused by Taylor and his contemporaries, man depends utterly upon Christ for his salvation because only Christ— being human and divine at once—can mediate between sinful man and an angry God, plead man's case as advocate before the bar of an infinite and offended Divine Justice, and so redeem man's debt to his Landlord by His own suffering death. But the idea of a "theanthropos" or "God-man" is not an easy one to grasp, and New England ministers devoted a good part of their preaching to trying to make their congregations understand it. Centuries of heresy regarding the precise relationship of the human and divine in Christ also made it necessary to reason most exactly. Taylor writes that "human faculties are as much too low to contain adequate conceptions of the Godhead as the Godhead is too high to be grasped by the little hand of human understanding" (C, 37), but he strives with his colleagues to close the gap. Most of the *Christographia* touches on the personal union of Christ's two natures, but the first three sermons speak about it most directly. The first points out that Christ's human nature was really human, although it was especially purified to be joined with the divine; the second demonstrates that Christ was also truly divine; and the third preaches the doctrine "That the divine nature and the human are personally united in Christ. Or, that the union between them is a personal union."

Unions are of different kinds, he reasons: physical or nonphysical. Obviously the union of natures in Christ is not physical, but nonphysical unions may be either "artificial" or "not artificial." He dismisses artificial unions (C, 78), and explains the inartificial as those that bind the things united by some special relationship involving no essential change in the things themselves: "And this sort of union is either common, as in a civil covenant and marriage compacts, or supernatural as to the institution of it, which is either visible, as our solemn and visible convenanting with God according to rules of the covenant of grace . . . or it is invisible . . . an union of our nature special to the head, and this is the personal union, whereby the two natures in our Lord Christ are joined together" (C, 78). By virtue of this invisible, special union, "Christ is as truly flesh as spirit; as properly mortal as immortal. No more rightly styled God than man; infinite than finite; almighty than weak; unchangeable than changeable; omniscient than nescient; omnipresent than confined" (C, 81). In other words, Christ has in his person all the properties of humanity and divinity together.

There is another kind of invisible union, not special but universal to "all members of the body of Christ mystical," the union between Christ and his church. Christ is to his elect as a head is to a body. The church and Christ make one eternal union: the body and head are mutually dependent; one without the other would be monstrous and unnatural. Taylor calls the elect saints the mystical body of Christ, and from this relationship springs the optimism in Taylor's theology: Christ is perfect only when all the members of his body are maintained together. "If Christ should have but one single child of God taken from him, he could not be complete or full." The fact that "Christ's body cannot lose its least member in its mystical nature" assures the saints that they will persevere in God's saving grace, for Christ hereby needs them as desperately as they need him. As long as any saint remains sinful, as long as any member of the mystical body remains corrupt, Christ must be unhealthy and his union with his body incomplete.

A third kind of union results from the personal one between Christ's human and divine natures, one Taylor calls "natural." In Christ himself, there is a transfer of divine properties to the human nature and of human properties to the divine. Were this not so, divinity could not suffer and die; and humanity could never acquire the spiritual and sanctifying influences necessary to carry on the work of prophet and priest. Christ would then be an inadequate Mediator. But Christ is not inadequate, the properties are transferable; and, furthermore, they may also be passed on to the saints, Christ's mystical body, through the church.

The Spirit of God tells us, Eph. 5:30, that we are members of his body, of his flesh, and of his bones. His manhood is of our manhood. . . . He is our . . .

near kinsman: so that there is a natural relation between his manhood and
ours; and hence, so long as his human nature remains in personal union to the
divine, there is this natural relation between Christ and his church. (C, 85)

But of course this union is eternal, and so the saints eternally have
access through the human nature they share with Christ to the divine
properties of light and grace which Christ's human nature possesses
through its hypostatic union with the Godhead. In Taylor's view, the
purified saint is united with Christ, and with Christ he shares the
divine wisdom of the Father.

Through these concepts of union, Taylor sees mankind most highly
honored and advanced in glory. This idea seems most unusual in a
Puritan, but it is reiterated in Taylor's prose and verse throughout his
professional career. In one of the earliest of the *Preparatory Meditations*
Taylor exults in the honor given to man over the angels: "I'll claim my
right: Give place ye angels bright." And the statement, the proud
exultation, is even stronger in the prose intended for the public:

Human nature is advanced as nigh to Deity, in its union unto the Deity in the
person of the Son of God, as created nature can be. . . . Oh! admirable. Give
place ye holy angels of light, ye sparkling stars of the morning. The brightest
glory, the highest seat in the kingdom of glory, the fairest colors in the
scutcheon of celestial honor, belong to my nature and not to yours. I cannot, I
may not allow it to you, without injury to mine own nature, and indignity and
ingratitude to my Lord, that hath assumed it into a personal conjunction with
his divine nature and seated it in the trinity (C, 25).

This statement is not simply a symptom of emotional enthusiasm; it is
a reasoned conclusion based upon the soundest theological assumptions. Its orthodoxy may be appreciated when we find the concept in
the writings of Increase Mather, who has long stood as the epitome of
New England Puritanism. In *The Mystery of Christ,* a book so much like
Taylor's *Christographia* that it may have served as a basis for Taylor's
sermons, Mather devotes the fourth sermon to the same doctrine—that
Christ's union with God is a personal union—and he actually works
with the same text as Taylor does in his third sermon: John 1:14: "The
Word was made Flesh." Mather, too, reasons that, because of Christ's
humanity, "we may be humbly familiar with the Lord Jesus, and with
God through Him. . . . He is become our near Kinsman."[44] He likewise agrees with Taylor that "That which does belong properly to the

Person of Christ is ascribed to either nature,"[45] and that, by virtue of the union of human and divine natures in the person of Christ, "Humane Nature is Dignifyed above any Created Nature."[46] But for Mather this conclusion does not yield the same intense joy it brings to Taylor. It is almost as if Mather were oblivious to the exciting implications of the idea; for Taylor the idea is charged with energy.

Indeed, Taylor carries the elevation of humankind so far as to see it "seated . . . in the trinity." This phrasing, which sounds as if Taylor were actually claiming to be deified or transformed into God, is common among the most noted mystics in the history of Christianity. To many it sounds like heresy; it is damnable because it represents the same kind of hubris or proud arrogance that led, in the first instance, to the fall of Adam and Eve; and it was described by Milton as the reason for Satan's banishment from heaven.[47] In the meditation accompanying Sermon III of the *Christographia* Taylor seems dangerously close to heresy in his proclamation:

> You holy angels, morning stars, bright sparks,
>   Give place: and lower your top gallants. Shew
> Your top-sail conjues to our slender barks:
>   The highest honor to our nature's due.
>   It's nearer Godhead by the Godhead made
>   Than yours in you that never from God stray'd.
>
> (*PM*, 2.44)

But Taylor, neither ignorant of the danger in such statement nor careless in his wording, guards himself from heresy by making a careful distinction in the same poem: "O! dignified humanity indeed: / Divinely person'd: almost deified."

Man is *almost* deified, but not quite; he is above the angels, but not yet God. Being created, he can never achieve Godhood, since God is by nature uncreated. Yet the honor accorded human nature in its union with Christ is greater than that accorded to any other nature: "Oh! then how is man's nature hereby advanced, when a body is prepared of it for the Son of God. Higher it cannot be, unless it could be deified. Created nature cannot be deified: but human nature is advanced as nigh to Deity, in its union unto the Deity in the person of the Son of God, as created nature can be" (*C*, 25).

What distinguishes Taylor's expression of this concept is, I think, his strong sense of personal involvement in what is, for others, only an abstract and relatively distant speculation. That is, Taylor conceived of "human nature" not as an abstraction but as the distinguishing quality of himself. He therefore, whether only metaphorically or actually, makes himself representative of the entire human race. This representation is especially clear in Meditation 2.77, where he traces the full cycle of humanity from original glory in Paradise to the fall into "this lowest pit more dark than night," to eventual elevation upon Christ's "golden chain of grace" back into "Glory's happy place." He uses the first person throughout, presenting himself as a bird with "Gold-fincht angel feathers"; but there is no doubt that the bird represents all humanity. Once we recognize this representative quality of Taylor's first person pronoun, we can more accurately appraise his most significant way of talking about the union between man and God: their marriage.

With deification, the Spiritual Marriage is, in mystical literature, perhaps the most frequent mode of describing the consummate union of the soul with God.[48] Especially those mystics who emphasize the personal nature of God are "forced in the end to acknowledge that the perfect union of Lover and Beloved cannot be suggested in the precise and arid terms of religious philosophy."[49] Underhill further explains: "It was natural and inevitable that the imagery of human love and marriage should have seemed to the mystic the best of all images of his own 'fulfillment of life'; his soul's surrender, first to the call, finally to the embrace of Perfect Love. It lay ready to his hand: it was understood of all men: and moreover, it certainly does offer, upon lower levels, a strangely exact parallel to the sequence of states in which man's spiritual consciousness unfolds itself, and which form the consummation of the mystic life."[50] Taylor's choice, therefore, of images of love, courtship, and marriage are quite traditional; these not only offer the strongest support to his place in the literature of mysticism but also provide the strongest defense against the accusation that his sensual and erotic imagery is somehow in opposition to his Puritan faith.

In this heavenly romance the soul of man is feminine; and she is pursued by Christ, who—we must remember—needs as greatly as man to consummate the union. Taylor's description of the game of love begins when he casts a furtive glance at Christ, who is coming to woo him: "I threw through Zion's lattice then an eye, / Which spi'd one like a lump of glory pure" (*PM*, 1.12). At this coy view of his coming Lover, Taylor bids his soul to "pine in love until this lovely one be thine." But his soul, ashamed of her own unworthiness, not only draws back in fear from the encounter but confesses her inadequacy in what is perhaps Taylor's most ardent passage:

> My lovely one, I fain would love thee much
> But all my love is none at all, I see,
> Oh! let thy beauty give a glorious touch
> Upon my heart, and melt to love all me.
> Lord melt me all up into love for thee
> Whose loveliness excells what love can be.
>
> (*PM*, 1.12)

At this point his soul, sensing the great distance between her capacity for love and the infinite love offered her by Christ, is often thrown into dejection. Teased by the view of beauty she cannot possibly possess, she is simultaneously encouraged and denied at this point of her spiritual progress, which is common to many mystics, and plunged into the "dark night of the soul" as Saint John of the Cross termed this stage. Taylor's soul cries in disappointment: "And shall the spiritual eye be wholly dark, / In th'heart of love, as not belov'd, condole?" (*PM*, 2.96). But Taylor mollifies her anguish, pointing out that the finite soul cannot expect, after all, to contain the infinite this side of heaven. Desiring all—Taylor tells her—

> Maybe thy measures are above thy might.
> Desires crave more than thou canst hold by far:
> If thou shouldst have but what thou would, if right,
> Thy pipkin soon would run o'er, break, or jar.
>
> (*PM*, 2.96)

He assures the soul that the lack of "love's evidence" is no sign that the love is wanting.

For we know that the Divine Lover is relentless, even militant, as we see in *God's Determinations;* and, even if the soul wished to avoid his love, she could not. He turns his eye of love upon her, and she surrenders: "Lord, let these charming glancing eyes of thine / Glance on my soul's bright eye its amorous beams" (*PM*, 2.119). And thus is love exchanged through the eyes. The eyes of the soul follow the beauty of Christ in the scriptures, the "rich love letter" from God to man.

But this visual exchange between the lovers focuses finally in their marriage, a circumstance so astonishing that Taylor never tires of ex-

pressing his amazement. The very first of the Meditations introduces
this as an image:

> What love is this of thine, that cannot be
> In thine infinity, O Lord, confin'd,
> Unless it in thy very person see
> Infinity, and finity conjoyn'd?
> What! hath thy Godhead, as not satisfied,
> Marri'd our manhood, making it its bride?

Just as in the union between Christ and God, there is an exchange of
properties, and what may be predicated of one may also be claimed for
the other; so it is in this marriage between Christ and the Soul: "What
strange appropriations hence arise? / Thy person mine, mine thine,
even weddenwise?" (*PM*, 2.79). But always Taylor marvels at the
miracle of his wedding to Christ: "Oh! matchless love, laid out on such
as he! / Should gold wed dung, should stars woo lobster claws, / It
would no wonder, like this wonder, cause" (*PM*, 2.33).

As it is cause for wonder, so it is cause for celebration—a wedding
feast to acknowledge the espousal of Christ and the soul. Preaching in
1694 on the text from Matthew 22, the parable of the feast, Taylor
exhorts his congregation to attend to its message: "It calls you, it
exhorts you, it salutes you with a fresh invitation unto the feast, saying
unto you, 'Come, Come. Come in, thou blessed of the Lord. Wherefore
standest thou without? Come in, and welcome. I have prepared room
for thee. . . . Oh, then come to the wedden' " (*TCLS*, 181). Over a
period of about a year, Taylor preached continually about the same
parable, interpreting the feast itself to be the Lord's Supper; but, from
the very beginning of the *Preparatory Meditations* to at least 1720, this
parable offered a source of feast and food imagery that Taylor plundered
frequently. In the poems he never comes to describe the marriage itself.
Its consummation, however, is another thing; it offers Taylor an unusual opportunity to describe the ecstasy of love. Fondling, kissing,
embracing, Christ ravishes his bride until she flies to Him "upon the
wings of ecstasies" (*PM*, 2.100), and is impregnated by her Lord.
Suggestions of pregnancy range from the most general images—a box
or cabinet or tabernacle in which something is placed—to somewhat
more suggestive images—as of a bowl or vessel filled with some fluid:
"O let thy lovely streams of love distill / Upon myself and spout their
spirits pure / Into my vial, and my vessel fill" (*PM* 2.32). Taylor carries

the sexual implications of the spiritual marriage considerably further than most writers who use it; and he does so consciously, for he takes full advantage of the conventional Christian ways of talking about the regeneration of the spirit, the birth of the New Man. Taylor explains, "The soul's the womb. Christ is the spermadote, / And saving grace the seed cast thereinto" (*PM* 2.80). He concludes: "When of this life my soul with child doth spring, / The babe of life swath'd up in grace shall sing."

Fulfilled by this pledge of renewed spiritual life, the "Daughters of Jerusalem" (by whom Taylor intends all unregenerate souls) are reassured:

> Whom Christ espouseth is his spouse indeed.
> His spouse or bride no single person, nay,
> She is an aggrigate so doth proceed
> And in it sure and can't be stole away.
> And if you thus be members made of me
> He'll be your bridegroom, you his spouse shall be.
>
> (*PM*, 2.132)

So we see in these last two lines that the soul of Taylor's spiritual marriage with Christ is at once both his own personal soul and the representative of all souls united in the Lord—the elect church.

In Meditation 2.133 Taylor is midway in a series of thirty-nine consecutive meditations upon his favorite book of the Old Testament— "The Song of Solomon"[51]—which he calls "Canticles." The most popular way to read "Canticles" was as an allegory of love between Christ and his church. Especially for mystical writers has this been a particularly attractive source of imagery; and among them was Saint Bernard, whose sermons on the "Cantica Canticorum" Taylor knew. Underhill suggests that "the mystic loved the Song of Songs because he there saw reflected, as in a mirror, the most secret experience of his soul."[52] We cannot, therefore, rely on Taylor's use of the first person pronoun as reference to himself alone. Even in those meditations where the representative quality is not obvious, we may not suppose that it is absent. What Taylor claims for his own experience is at the same time the collective experience of all the elect through all time.

Taylor becomes increasingly passionate in his poetry as he grows older. From the age of seventy on and when he is concentrating almost exclusively on the Song of Songs, he treats the spiritual marriage more

and more amorously. His very last meditation begins, in fact, with the
ardent "Heart sick my Lord, heart sick of love to thee!" And he claims
in 1714 to have been brought "up in a trance" by Christ's "amorous
chains" (*PM*, 2.120).

The entranced mystic is most familiar to the popular mind through
the frequent portrayals of Saint Teresa and Saint Francis frozen in
ecstatic agony at the moment of union with Christ. The end of the
mystic progress has come to be viewed as the complete loss of the
senses—as absolute oblivion to the immediate world. And this view has
been abetted by the great debate from the Middle Ages on between the
advantages of the life of pure contemplation over that of action. But the
most notable mystics were hardly perpetual solitaries: Saint Teresa,
Saint Francis of Assisi, Saint Catherine of Siena, Saint Ignatius Loyola,
George Fox, Saint Bernard of Clairvaux, Saint Joan of Arc—and for
that matter, Saint John the Evangelist and Saint Paul—all were reform-
ers, some on an international scale; founders of hospitals and religious
orders; military leaders and teachers. Vigorously engaged in the business of living, they were men and women of superb energy, discipline,
and efficiency who were unafraid of this world and who were distinguished by their attempts to grapple with it. Except for some orientals
and especially the Buddhist, the highest mystical attainment results in
an active, though changed, worldly life.[53]

So with Taylor, building a world at the westernmost limit of the
Massachusetts Bay Colony, there was not time, occasion, nor desire to
withdraw from carrying out God's will in mundane affairs. Taylor
assumed that the spiritual life and the natural life went together, that
the transformation brought about by the birth of the New Man is
evidenced "in holy conversation" or behavior. Again and again in the
Christographia, Taylor tries to tell his frontier congregation what the
unitive life means. He calls it, as Thomas à Kempis does, the Imitation
of Christ. Through the mystical union—whether by the immediate
elevation of one's own soul through the stages Taylor traces in his own
writing, or through the more conventional admission to full membership in Christ's mystical body—one gains access to the properties of the
Godhead. These properties—life, grace, truth, and wisdom—are reflected in the Christ-like life of those who attain them. The Godly gifts
are not merely for appreciation but for use.

The duty to "improve all the talents thus derived" is, then, the
philosophical root of Taylor's entire life; and it was more fully revealed
to Taylor's consciousness than the bases of lives usually are even to very

alert and self-conscious persons. But we have to view Taylor's concept as he understood it before we can judge its fruits, his poetry. It is a mystical root that proceeds through various stages so conventional that histories and descriptions of the mystical process seem to have been written with Taylor in mind. It proceeds from the awakening of the self to a real awareness of God, which is marked both by a conviction of personal sinfulness and by an illumination of his understanding regarding the nature of ultimate reality. Once converted, Taylor moves through almost ascetic self-struggle to reach a state of purification from sin; and he exercises his whole being in the arduous mental discipline of meditation. This exercise occasionally yields visions, or it at least results in the active use of the imagination that finds expression in his poetry. He passes beyond these, finally, to a state of complete mystical union with Christ—he is elevated above all created things, nearly deified. This union he can only describe in terms of holy wedlock; and he reflects this union, or strives to, in the imitation of Christ.

Recognizing how fruitful the mystical literary tradition was for Taylor does not require believing that he made any claims to personal mysticism. Taylor did see very clearly the parallel character of mysticism with the ordinary pattern of redemptive experience. Speaking for the representative soul, Taylor used the contemplative way to intensify more ordinary Protestant religious experiences. The patterns remain useful abstractions, but the emotion they call upon and the language that emotion generates are everywhere singular and highly personal. The very first *Meditation* supposes in its marriage imagery that the mystical union has been accomplished; thirty years later Taylor is still bewailing his "hide-bound heart" for resisting the loveliness of Christ, suggesting the union has never been consummated. In between, self-revilings and near-deification occur side by side. Indeed, if read as personal poems, Taylor's *Meditations,* for all their ardent longing, never attain a beatified state, and remain a dismaying record of spiritual frustration and failure. Dean Inge observes that the mystic "strives to reach its end, but the end being an infinite one, no process can reach it."[54] To the representative soul, however, the mystical process is a *progressus ad infinitum,* and Taylor's expression of it must, therefore, be repetitious and unending; all its stages must be uttered throughout his entire life.

Chapter Three
From Preacher to Poet

John Donne and Richard Baxter were powerful preacher-poets. Naturally their poems share certain verbal and mental characteristics with their sermons, but those poems do not depend upon the sermons in any close or necessary way. With Edward Taylor the case is quite different, for his poems lose their full import if divorced from his sermons. Only sixty-two sermons—two versions of the 1679 Foundation-Day presentation, two disciplinary sermons from 1713, the fourteen of the *Christographia,* eight in the *Treatise,* and the thirty-six recently discovered Sacrament-Day sermons called *Upon the Types of the Old Testament*— are extant of the nearly three thousand Taylor must have preached; but they are sufficient to evidence the uncommon unity of his teaching and his artistic life. The sermons stand as indispensable commentary upon the poetry, for they are often veritable worksheets for the poems.

Formally, these sermons are typical of the New England Puritan: Taylor begins by citing a scriptural text, which he briefly explicates or "opens." What the explication reveals is summarized in a pithy proposition called the "Doctrine," which is the main truth inferred from a particular text. The body of the sermon—contrary to the practice of some of his contemporaries—is an extensive proof of this doctrine, a fact which again underlines the intellectual emphasis of Taylor's faith.[1] He reduces his proofs to Ramist method, for he divides and subdivides and then numbers each head and subhead of his topic but seldom allows more than a page or two to each unit of thought. This method results in clear distinctions and in a fairly clear progress of thought, but it also chops the sermon into such small units that graceful writing never extends beyond a page or two at a time.

Taylor spends anywhere from half to two-thirds of his sermon proving the doctrine, and then he applies or "improves" it for the congregation. In this application he observes a conventional division into a series of "Uses" to which the doctrinal truth may be put. These are ordinarily four: the use by way of information or inference, in which Taylor points out the consequences of the truth he has just demonstrated or draws corollary truths; the use by way of reproof, in which those who do not accept the doctrine are shown to jeopardize their salvation; the use by way of consolation, in which Taylor assures those who accept his proof that they have thereby climbed one more rung up the ladder to bliss; and, finally, the use by way of exhortation, where Taylor urges sinners to repent and saints to persevere in the acceptance of this doctrine.

Because these sermons allow us to see Taylor at work as a writer more clearly than does the poetry alone, they, generally, provide interesting insights into Taylor's style and thought; and, more particularly, they develop images and ideas that from time to time appear in the poems. Addressed to a single representative or collective soul (like the "I" of the *Meditations*), the sermons are kinds of extended soliloquies. They reflect Taylor's fondness for exempla, allegory, and illustrious providences; and they sometimes explain the symbolism of the poetry. For example, his sermon "A Particular Church is God's House" uses the central image of a house in which God will dwell. Christ is the cornerstone; the saints are the stones of which the superstructure is built; and the church covenant cements them together. These are commonplace figures which need no explanation; but early in the sermon he considers the furnishings for this house and the utensils to be placed in it. These include golden candlesticks, altars, incense, and sacrificial fire—strange furniture for a Puritan temple. But Taylor clearly explains that the altar represents the person and merits of Christ; the incense, the prayers of the saints; and the fire, "the holy flame of heavenly affection" (*UW*, 1:288–89). Taylor's use, then, of the details of the Old Testament ceremony in his poetry is no sign at all that, as some early critics and historians implied, he finds the high Anglican or the Catholic church service more attractive than the Congregational.

But the *Christographia* sermons most fully illustrate how Taylor's prose influenced his poetry. The *Christographia* is Taylor's only collection of Sacrament-Day sermons, which, besides being the most basic statement of his Christology, are also the most intimately related to his verse. He wrote them at about six-week intervals; and then, after completing each one but before delivering it, he composed the poetic meditation. The sermon is the dry, ratiocinative discourse which analytically demonstrates the great admirableness of Christ; the poem is Taylor's private response to his own exhortation, a statement of raised affections cast in the form of a colloquy with Christ.

The clue both to the order of composition of the sermon and poem and to the relationship of the two lies in the subtitle Taylor penned to the *Preparatory Meditations*. He says the poems are based "chiefly upon the doctrine preached upon the day of administration" and that they were written before his approach to the Lord's Supper. Now, if they were based upon the "doctrine" preached on that day, it must at least have been chosen before the poem was written; and this, by the way, obviates the problem of trying to relate the meditations to their scriptural texts. Many readers are disturbed by the fact that the poems often seem completely unrelated to the scriptural passages that function as epigraphs to the poems. Meditation 6, First Series, for example, begins with the text from Cant. 2:1: "I am the lily of the valleys." But the central image of the poem concerns the minting of a gold coin, the poet's soul, upon which Taylor petitions of the Lord's image to be stamped; and there is no flower imagery at all. The problem of explaining the apparent lack of connection would be solved, of course, if we had the sermon accompanying this poem; for then we should have the doctrine itself—the central proposition that Taylor proves in the sermon—and its relationship to the poem would presumably be quite clear. Usually, because the doctrine and the text of the sermons are so similar, this problem does not arise.

In the *Christographia*, where sermons and poems do match, their relationship is inescapable. Not only does the sermon usually call the poem into being (ordinarily in the exhortation) but it also presents the subject, provides both the central and subordinate images, and sometimes even dictates the logical order in which the poem develops. Moreover, the sermon opens avenues of inference that the poem ignores completely; it restates more clearly what the compression of the poetry seems to overlook; and it supplies details necessary to a full, accurate understanding of the poem. And, most significantly, the sermon provides the larger contexts of Taylor's thought in which the poem belongs.[2]

This dependence of the poems upon the sermons probably holds for the majority of Taylor's *Meditations*. Since we do not have most of the sermons for these poems, our understanding of them must remain something less than complete. And, consequently, our appreciation of Taylor's poetic workmanship is limited to the extent that we can apply what we know from the extant sermons to other poems. But because of the underlying unity springing from Taylor's mysticism and because the sermons we do have are so crucial to his thought, the extent to which they can be applied is great indeed. However, Taylor's teachings regarding the Lord's Supper and the direct influence of his preaching upon his poems do not indicate alone the influence of his mysticism in his poetic life; for his theory of poetry was derived from his mysticism.

The relationship of poetry—or, for that matter, any of the arts—to mysticism is traditionally close. The mystic, transcending the world of sense to achieve union with God, has had an actual experience for which his vocabulary—even his categories of perception, understanding, and discursive reason—are inadequate. The fullness of his experience is not only inexpressible in the propositions of literal language but also logically unthinkable. To reduce the ineffable experience to something tangible enough to be grasped and retained in the understanding, he must find a symbol or set of symbols to stand for that experience— some mechanism by which he can conceive and order his utterly new cognition and with which he can express and so communicate his experience to others. For this reason, all discussions of mysticism become, at their most profound, symbolic; and always, because the whole human complex is involved in the experience, these symbols serve affectively or emotionally as well as intellectually. In fact, the symbolism is designed not so much to assist communication or discourse as it is to make possible the formulation of new concepts.

This describes exactly the function of symbols in poetry; for the problem facing the articulate mystic and the poet is identical. Poets, painters, musicians, sculptors, architects, and even mathematicians and scientists, when considering the creative act that brings them to new formulations or concepts or works, fall irresistibly into the language of search, vision or insight, and expression. The sociologist— tracing what the modern poet thinks he himself does or actually experiences in the act of creating a poem—also finds a pattern suspiciously parallel to that of the mystical experience. And the philosopher, working in most unmystical terms, comes likewise to the language of vision to explain artistic creativity.[3] Each sees the artist transcending somehow—by effort, by chance, by force—the world of normal sense and thought to a perception of something "beyond." This "beyond" is always expressed differently, but the expression always assumes that truth or reality lies ultimately outside the world of normal sense experience—or at least that area of experience covered by our vocabulary. It further assumes that through discipline the artist actually attains a "sight" or intuition of this ultimate reality and, finally, that the materials of the world of sense may be manipulated, shaped, and formed to express the new insight.

Behind these attempts to analyze creativity lies the faith that art involves a truly creative act; that this act is a way of truth independent of science and its disciplines, independent even of reason (though not inconsistent with reason); and that the act is, therefore, a most important human activity. Largely because of the conception of the artist as creator, recent books about the relationship of theology and literature have without fail devoted a chapter to mysticism, in which the author indicates the inescapableness of the connection. Two points of connection have received considerable attention: one has been the theory that the artist is divinely inspired; the other, more amenable to modern critics, generally follows Coleridge and finds the creative faculty itself—the imagination—"a repetition in the finite mind of the eternal act of creation in the infinite I AM."[4]

Both notions of divine inspiration and the creative act entered Taylor's thought; but, not primarily interested in the speculative side of this problem and limited by the aesthetic principles of his own time, he never very systematically developed his theories. Throughout his prose and poetry he nonetheless drops frequent judgments about art and nature; the art of creation; beauty; the function of poetry; the nature of language and metaphor; the limits of the imagination; and his own motives for writing. He even offers some criticism of his own poetic efforts. Assembled, these comments delineate a most useful, if not startlingly original, conception of the art of poetry.

In the first place, the writing of poetry was to Taylor a religious act in two ways: the first rather subtle, the second fairly obvious. The first begins with Taylor's understanding of the meaning of "reason," which he defined from the two "principles" inherent in it. The first of these is "internal," according to which reason is simply "the exercise of that faculty or power of the soul, discursively, which inseparably cleaves unto the mind of God: Hence it is in all men. This power doth from its very essence adhere to the mind of the Almighty, and wherein its exercise is not conformable to the mind of God, willingly conscience accuseth, and wherein it fails thereof thrô ignorance, conscience excuses" (TCLS, 61). This congruity of the human with the divine mind is impossible while man is in a state of sin, and so there could be no reason if all depended upon this internal principle. God has therefore provided reason with an external principle, which Taylor explains: "Now the will of God is revealed unto us more obscurely, as in the law of nature and of the creation. For there stands imprinted upon the nature of the creature a declaration of the will of God in suitableness of one part unto another: and of one thing unto another. So also in the disposal and management of the whole, and of each part." Reason in this statement means consistency with natural order; but a second external principle is also presented: God also reveals his will "in the law of grace and Holy Scriptures. This is given out graciously, to regulate the principle internal in its exercise, now being blinded by sin, and that in order to his recovery from sin principally. So that reason is the exercise of that internal principle of adherence unto God's will discursively, according to the external rule revealing the same. Now where the discourse is not conformable to this rule (whether the discourse is mental or vocal), it is not reason, but unreasonableness and sophistry" (*TCLS*, 61).

In Taylor's terms, one reasons correctly when one first sees things as God actually intended them to be seen and then applies the correct name to them. Correct naming of objects of experience is a sign of wisdom, Taylor argues; for he assumes that in the order of the universe the connection between words and the things they signify is a God-ordained, immutable one. His conception of the absolute nature of this relationship between language and nature is revealed in Taylor's description of Adam's wisdom in paradise.

"O the light with which Adam's soul was filled," exclaims Taylor. "It must needs be great, and the rectitude of his will answerable. Otherwise it could not have been according to the majesty of infinite wisdom to have left with him the giving of names to the creatures that were created by him [Christ]. For had not his light discovered their very natures, and his delight have been to name things according to their natures, he might have called light 'darkness' and darkness 'light'; life 'death,' and death 'life'; heat 'coldness,' and cold 'heat'; a man a 'brute,' and a brute a 'man,' etc." (*C*, 209). He does not spell out what the consequences of this universal misnomer would have been, but he implies it would have been catastrophic.

Language is the symbol of thought to Taylor; and, if language is inaccurate or inadequate or unsuitable, it bespeaks a failure of thought and reason, or, in the last analysis, a want of wisdom. Simply to articulate sounds and put them together with stress and intonation is not, in itself, to speak. There must also be truth in the sounds: "Words oral but thoughts whiffled in the wind. / If written only inked paper be. / Unless truth mantle, they bely the mind" (*PM*, 2.158). This idea Taylor repeats several times, always emphasizing the necessary connection between words and thoughts. "Words mental are syllabicated

thoughts; / Words oral but thoughts whiffled in the wind" (*PM* 2.43).
Consequently the *Preparatory Meditations* frequently reiterate the want
of words proceeding from a want of reason or wisdom or thought:

> My only dear, dear Lord, I search to find
> My golden ark of thought, thoughts fit and store:
> And search each till and drawer of my mind
> For thoughts full fit to deck thy kindness o'er,
> But find my forehead empty of such thoughts
> And so my words are simply ragged, nought.
>
> (*PM*, 2.141)

There are thus two reasons why Taylor so often laments his own
failure of language in the meditations. The first is not because his
vocabulary is particularly limited, but because his subject is beyond the
compass of human reason. This limitation he makes explicit in both
prose and poetry: "Human faculties are as much too low to contain
adequate conceptions of the Godhead as the Godhead is too high to be
grasped by the little hand of human understanding" (*C*, 37). In another
instance, writing of the all-fullness of the Godhead as it appears in
Christ, he states: "It doth as far exceed created understanding to produce any full answer thereto, as the all fullness of Godhead doth exceed
the capacity of the created understanding to contain it" (*C*, 145). Of
the union of Christ's two natures in one person, Taylor preaches, "it is
so singular a work, there is not so much as a shadow of it to be found in
the creation to enlighten our conception in the same. Reason cannot
portray out the same. All the light in the eye of reason is not so much as
can make out a little glimmering thereof in the soul" (*C* 23–24). It is,
he concludes, a matter of faith, not of definition.

In poetry, the same attitude finds expression even more clearly:

> Things styled transcendent do transcend the style
> Of reason. Reason's stairs ne'er reach so high.
> But Jacob's golden ladder rungs do foil
> All reason's strides, wrought of THEANTHROPIE.
>
> (*PM*, 2.44)

Even more explicitly in the poem just preceding this, he defines this
difficulty: "Words, though the finest twine of reason, are / Too coarse a
web for deity to wear" (*PM*, 2.43). And the reason is pretty clear.
Human reason, unaided by saving grace, is thoroughly confused and

unreliable regarding things of this world, to say nothing of the transcendent truths of religion. Because human thoughts are "filthy fumes that smoke / From smutty huts," the hut itself must be purified before the poet can speak truth. And what makes the hut smutty in the first place we can easily imagine—sin: "Thou art a golden theme," Taylor says to his Lord,

> but I am lean,
> A leaden orator upon the same.
> Thy golden web excells my dozy beam:
> Whose linsey-woolsey loom deserves thy blame.
> It's all defiled, unbiassed too by sin.
>
> *(PM,* 1.26)

The true poet, then, must be inspired in a sense—filled with the spirit of the Lord—actually filled with saving grace. Without such gracious illumination of his intellectual faculty, his judgment, his understanding, and his will, the poet can do no more than darken the glory of his theme.

> What shall I say, my dear, dear Lord, most dear
> Of thee? My choicest words, when spoke, are then
> Articulated breath, soon disappear.
> If wrote, are but the drivel of my pen,
> Beblacked with my ink, soon worn out unless
> The Holy Spirit be their inward dress.
>
> *(PM,* 2.142)

As one might readily suspect, the poet only wastes his time invoking the classical Muses. In one of his earliest poems—written before he came to New England and when, as a student of languages, he was deeply involved in classical literature—Taylor begins with an invocation to all nine Muses. But when he observes the convention later, it is always to contrast his Muse with the true source of inspiration, Christ. "Fain would I brighten bright thy glory," he says to Christ, "but / Do fear my Muse will thy bright glory smoot" *(PM,* 2.123B). He naturally turns to Christ to correct his want of reason and want of words:

> Lord, dub my tongue with a new tier of words
> More comprehensive far than my dull speech,

> That I may dress thy excellency, Lord,
> In language welted with emphatic reach.
>
> (*PM*, 2.19)

He petitions the Lord to inspire him most directly: "Be thou my head, and act my tongue, whereby / Its tittle-tattle may thee glorify" (*PM*, 2.37). Sometimes he invokes inspiration by wishing that he had for a pen a quill plucked from the wings of an angel (*PM* 2.60B); that he were enriched with "seraphic life" (*PM*, 2.72); or that Christ would implant in his heart "Each sanctifying garden grace" (*PM*, 2.145). While he never banishes the Muses—nor supplants them with the heavenly Muse Urania, as Milton and many English writers did—Taylor seems to have felt them unnecessary, inappropriate, or perhaps only inefficacious.

Of course, what Taylor speculates to be the right relationship of words, reason, wisdom, and grace to the poet's divine subject is equally applicable to anyone—poet or not—who seeks to praise God. In one meditation, for example, Taylor joins the minister or divinity scholar and the poet together in the same task of celebrating the Lord's mysterious ways. This does not indicate that in Taylor's mind the poet and divine are confused, or that he thinks that one must be a divine in order to be a poet. But it does emphasize the similarity of their problems and their limitations, and it indicates his own full awareness of the fact that as a poet he writes largely to define and explain, as a minister would do.

This similarity of function is further affirmed in Taylor's frequent descriptions of himself in his poetry as an orator; and, in fact, most of his statements regarding reason and words and thoughts grow from this image. Taylor seems in this attitude to be in agreement with most of his contemporaries; for they, as Professor Miller says, were trained in the Ramist principles of rhetoric as well as logic, and they believed that "verse was simply a heightened form of eloquence, it was speech more plenteously ornamented with tropes and figures than prose, but still speech; like the oration, its function was to carry . . . arguments from man to man."[5] We have already seen Taylor call himself a lean and leaden orator upon a golden and transcendent theme. Elsewhere he describes his poetic function in much the same way:

> The orator from rhetoric gardens picks
>   His spangled flowers of sweet-breathed eloquence
> Wherewith his oratory brisk he tricks,

> Whose spicy charms ear jewels do commence.
> Shall bits of brains be candied thus for ears?
> My theme claims sugar candied far more clear.
>
> *(PM,* 2.44)

According to the theory of the times, the main body of oratory was "dialectic," including the acts of invention, of memory, and of disposition of matter. Rhetoric tended to include ornamentation and exornation, elocution, and delivery; its specific purpose was to ornament the oration, and this seems to agree with Taylor's conception, where, as in the poem quoted above, he seeks in poetry to decorate or ornament, tricking out the sense of his speech with jeweled earrings.

Ornamentation is largely the basis of Taylor's poetry, and Taylor frankly views it as a mode of decorating the transcendent truths of his faith.

> Thoughts, though the fairest blossoms of my mind,
> Are things too loose and light t'strew at the gate
> Of thy bright palace. My words hence are wind
> Moulded in print up thee to decorate.
>
> *(PM,* 2.141)

And a few lines later he confesses that Christ's love for his spouse is beyond even the rhetorical power of angels to dress it out. Favorite among images of decoration or ornament for Taylor is that of a beautiful robe or gown with which Christ's truth is dressed or made more attractive. The notion of a poet as a weaver of a lovely cloth appears most early in Taylor; for sometime before 1668 probably, when Taylor was still living in England, he sent an affectionate letter in verse to one whom he identifies only as "my schoolfellow, W. M." (no one with these initials was at Harvard between 1668 and 1671 while Taylor was there); and he concluded it with these lines:

> What though my Muse be not adorned so rare
> As Ovid's golden verses do declare
> My love: yet it is in the loom tied
> Where golden quills of love weave on the web.
> Which web I take out of my loom and send
> It, as a present unto you, my friend,
> But though I send the web, I keep the thrum
> To draw another web up in my loom.[6]

With somewhat different implications, the weaving image culmi-
nates finally in Taylor's best known poem "Huswifery," but it is a
common figure of his thought. Nearing graduation from Harvard in
1671, the members of the senior class met in the College Hall on 5 May
to present their final declamations. Taylor explains the proceedings:
"Four declaimed in the praise of four languages, and five upon the five
senses. Those upon the languages declaimed in the language they
treated of, and hence mine ran in English." But it seems not to have
been an unwelcome division of topics to Taylor, for he wrote 212 lines
of heroic couplets with considerable gusto and with some of the heavy
humor that marks Milton's "Prolusions." He begins with the hope that
his auditors will not expect the sweetness of a heated fancy in his
discourse; for, as he apologizes, "no such flowers grow / Within my
garden; no such spirits flow / From mine alembick, neither have I skill /
To rain such honey falls out of my still" (11.15–22). Then, as if
concluding a dramatic scene, he recalls his main purpose: "But why
stand I thus rapping at the door? / I'll draw the latch, and in, and rap
no more" (11.33–34).

Once "in," he introduces the robe image almost immediately.
Speech, "the crystal chariot where the mind in progress rides," is the
holiday attire of human thought.[7]

> Now that speech wealthiest is, whose curious web
> Of finest twine is wrought, nor cumbered
> With knots, galls, ends, or thumbs, but doth obtain
> All golden rhetoric to trim the same.
>
> (11.49–52)

The yarn with which English is woven is distinguished for its grammatical simplicity—its lack of the encumbrances of a multiplicity of cases
and declensions. Moreover, compounded of the most useful words and
sounds of Hebrew, Latin, and Greek, woven together with the proverbs
of all tongues to make a cloth of gold (11.55–140), it combines richly
with other yarns. Rhetoric then appears to enhance the language:

> Our web thus wrought, rich rhetoric steps in
> As golden lace a silver web to trim.
> There's scarce a single thrid but doth entwine
> A trope or figure in't to make it fine.
> Here lies a metonymy; there doth skulk

> An irony; here underneath this bulk
> A metaphor; synecdoche doth rear
> And open publicly shop windows here.
> These and their offspring their affections spend
> Our Lady English to court and tend.
> Of swashy figures, too, there throngs in store
> Her dressing to emblanch and broider o'er,
> And first decks words and sounds where jiming feet
> Of measured steps with symphony run sweet,
> Clothing our English Muse in poetry
> Whose warbling melody let them descry,
> Whose light souls in their fingers' ends to caper
> And dance on ropes with curtsies to the quaver.
>
> (11.141–58)

Poetry as speech fancified seems to be Taylor's sole view. The next few lines enumerate particular decorations—the figures of sound and sense that poetry makes use of, all "set and spread / Like to mosaic work all o'er our web."

The web, woven of English yarn, intertwined with the borrowings from other languages, and decorated with poetry is a kind of "English huswifery," says Taylor, a satin cloth fit "to set / Forth majesty in ev'ry single jet." This last refers directly not to setting out the majesty of Christ but that of human thought. Since, however, the highest of human thoughts concern the mysteries of Christ, the union of natures, and the redemption, the robe of English seems to fit these as appropriately as it does thought in general. On the whole, though Taylor's may be a noble view of speech, it is rather a low view of poetry.

But Taylor's declamation is, after all, a college exercise; and it should not be surprising that it offers only a superficial view. In one way it has implications of significant scope; that is, the sartorial notion of speech as a cloth for thought necessarily in time brings Taylor to a sense of symbolism that enriches his poetic theory, though he never articulates that theory. And more directly, it offers him a ready metaphor to put to work in his own poetry.

> Had I angelic skill and on their wheel
> Could spin the purest white silk into
> The finest twine and then the same should reel
> And weave't a satin web therein also
> Or finest taffity with shines like gold

And decked with precious stones, brightest to behold,
And all inwrought with needle work most rich
    Even of the Holy Ghost to lap up in,
My heart full freight with love refined, the which
    Up on thy glorious self I ever bring
And for thy sake thy all fair spouse should wear't.
                                                              (*PM*, 2.147)

By 1718, when he wrote this poem, the web of speech functioned in a much more complex manner than it did at first: it covers Christ and then, because Christ and his spouse are one, it is made to drape the spouse—probably the church—but, because of the ambivalent meaning of the spouse as either the church or Taylor himself, it may also be a glorious robe for himself.

Had Taylor ever undertaken to compose an extended poetics, I think it doubtful that he would have produced a significant treatise. Certainly his intellectual capability would not have disqualified him, nor would his quickness of wit and obvious sensitivity to beauty have done so. But, accepting the basic Ramist view that rhetoric itself is the dressing of oratory and that poetry is the "tricking out" of that dressing, he could not, I think, have progressed from that position to the profound understanding of poetic symbolism that stretches from Plato through Coleridge and Emerson to modern theorists. In this sense, it is true that Puritanism impeded the development of a serious art and philosophy of poetry—not simply because religious sternness forbade exciting the affections, as many critics and historians have too easily said, but because the Puritans turned to an educator whose system removed poetry from a serious position to an adventitious one. Certainly the Puritans in their faith generally, and in their theology specifically, were not unsophisticated in their symbolic theory, as Robert Daly has demonstrated.

Basically, Taylor's view of symbols is twofold, as may be seen in his comments about metaphor. When his intention is humbly to compare the best he can do with the glory of his Lord, he minimizes the nature and function of metaphor; he makes it a tassel on the robe of speech: "Should all quaint metaphors teem ev'ry bud / Of sparkling eloquence upon the same, / It would appear as dawbing pearls with mud" (*PM*, 1.13). Even if he works as purely as it is possible for a human being to work, the gift of poetry he can present must be a poor one: "packed of gilded nonsense," "dull tacklings tag'd / With ragged nonsense" (*PM*

2.35, 36). This represents, however, only one view of metaphor; the other is more dignified.

The dignity arises, appropriately, from his consideration of the personal union of the divine and human natures in Christ. Contending that both natures are united in one person, he offers several arguments to the effect that anything one can say about one nature is equally applicable to the other (*C*, 128–29). In this fashion Taylor justifies a kind of anthropomorphizing of God and transcendent reality, which accounts in large part for his domesticating divine actions, for his reducing the most noble and magnificent metaphysical facts to kitchen images—the source of both surprise and delight in Taylor's poetry. Because the union is real and eternal, the individual soul—or the representative elected soul—which is Christ's spouse may be described most legitimately as carrying on the tasks of an ordinary human housewife; and the cleaning, spinning and weaving, and preparing meals are all metaphorically applicable to the relationship of Christ and the soul.

To conceive thus of the hypostatical union is not adequate to the fact of that union itself, he admits. But, he adds: "It is above the contemplation and reach of men or angels to describe this union as it is. That small account . . . given of it is like unto our shallow and dark understandings, and though we conceive of it in some respect thus, yet we cannot come to it thereby" (*C*, 103). To admit that metaphorical speech is not suitable to transcendent reality itself is not, however, to admit that it is a lie and should not be used. Some means must be found for grasping transcendent reality, and for this metaphor works. In the first place, "Words are used only to import the intent in the mind of the speaker. And all languages admit of metaphorical forms of speech . . . And this sort of speech never was expected to be literally true, nor charged to be a lying form of speech, but a neat, rhetorical, and wise manner of speaking. Hence said God's Spirit in the Psalmist, Ps. 49:3–4, 'I will open my mouth in wisdom: the meditation of my heart shall be of understanding. I will encline mine ear to a parable and open my dark saying upon my harp.' Hence then this form of speech is a truth-speaking form, conveying the thoughts of the heart of the speaker unto the hearers in such words as are apt to do it metaphorically and wisely" (*C*, 273). This is certainly to give symbolic import to metaphors, which, as Yeats suggests, "are not profound enough to be moving, when they are not symbols, and when they are symbols, they are the most perfect of all. . . ."[8]

Taylor continues to defend this view elsewhere. He maintains that

there is between worldly and spiritual things a correspondence that not
only permits one to talk of spiritual matters in natural terms but is the
only way some spiritual matters can be discussed. "Natural things are
not unsuitable to illustrate supernaturals by. For Christ in his parables,
doth illustrate supernatural things by natural, and if it were not thus,
we could arrive at no knowledge of supernatural things. For we are not
able to see above naturals. God hath a sweet harmony of reason running
the same throughout the whole creation, even through every distinct
sort of creatures, hence Christ on this very account makes use of natural
things to illustrate supernaturals by . . . and the Apostle argues invisible things from the visible . . ." (TCLS, 43). Thus Christ becomes a
poet by reducing supernatural matters through metaphor to bring them
within the scope of human understanding, thereby sanctioning Taylor's
doing the same.

Christ as an artist appears with reasonable frequency in Taylor's
poetry, but it is usually in His creative capacity. In Meditation 2.50
He carves a box out of pure pearl, so creating the first man; and, when
the beautiful box falls and breaks, "The artist puts his glorious hand
again / Out to the work," In Meditation 2.78, Christ, working out the
plan of man's redemption, is described thus: "Yet in the upper room of
paradise / An artist anvill'd out relief, sure good." But most significantly for Taylor's theory of poetry is Christ as the poet, who appears in
two meditations. Both of these are among the last ones of Taylor's
career, and both are about Taylor's favorite "Canticles." Meditation
2.151 comments on the allegory of Cant. 7:4, in which, as Taylor reads
it, Christ is singing the praises of his spouse, comparing her neck to an
ivory tower, her eyes to beautiful fish pools, and her nose to the alert
tower of Lebanon as it "smells the actions of Christ's enemy." Each of
these comparisons is a metaphor, says Taylor, after elaborately rehears-
ing them. What the reader must do is "spiritualize" and moralize the
metaphors—see them symbolically, in other words, until the intent of
the speaker, Christ the poet, is made clear. In this case, the metaphors
designate that Christ's spouse is most dear but has enemies from whom
she must be protected.

Taylor continues his view of Christ as distilling silver metaphors and
tropes, divine rhetoric upon his spouse: "Thou gildest o'er with sparkling metaphors / The object thy eternal love fell on"(PM, 2.152). In
this poem the two views of metaphor seem to coalesce. That is, metaphor is treated as Taylor treats it rhetorically—a decoration, a shiny
varnish used to beautify its object. But at the same time we know that

the varnish has to be spiritualized and moralized, that it is a symbolic varnish used by the most glorious of poets to express what otherwise could not be accommodated to human understanding. Thus "Canticles" sanctions the writing of poetry. Moreover, since Taylor always preaches that the holy life is imitative of the life of Christ, here he has Christ the glorious orator to emulate in his poetry. In so emulating Christ, Taylor is, in a way, making the writing of poetry a religious act; he is repeating finitely "the eternal act of creation in the infinite I AM." This—plus the necessity of saving grace to the poet's intellectual faculty and of inspiration from Christ—constitutes, I think, the rather more subtle way in which poetry is a religious act to Taylor.

But on a far more obvious level, Taylor thought of his poetry as a religious duty, especially in his *Preparatory Meditations* in which he reasons that men owe honor to those who honor them most. No one has honored man more than Christ did in assuming a human nature and in elevating man above the angels. For this reason, man has the constant obligation literally to sing God's glory as the rest of nature does. In this sense, Taylor's motive was the same as Anne Bradstreet's in "Contemplations."[9] In a world where natural objects sing God's praises simply by being what they are, converted men and angels are obliged "to give the revenue of praise to God on the account of the works of creation. The whole creation doth bring all its shining glory as a sacrifice to be offered up to God from and upon the altar of the rational creature in sparkling songs of praises to God" (*C,* 312).

This conception of man as the singer of the creation was not only fairly popular but practiced a good deal. Jonathan Edwards makes bursting into song characteristic of a true Christian, and we know that he frequently roamed the fields and woods singing God's praises aloud. And Richard Baxter, who thought, "Sure there is somewhat of Heaven in Holy Poetry," remembered late in life that "It was not the least comfort that I had in the converse of my late dear Wife, that our first in the Morning, and last in Bed at Night, was a Psalm of Praise (till the hearing of others interrupted it.)"[10] When Taylor says of his poetry, "I'll bring unto thine altar th'best of all / My flock affords" (*PM,* 1.21), he too indicates clearly that his meditations are part of his religious duty and a sacrificial offering to Christ.

This sacrifice to Christ is not always made easily; for devotional writers constantly called for devotees to shoot sighs, groans, and tears to God—ejaculatory prayers expressing love, sorrow, gratitude, or praise. These brief prayers were not performed at set times but whenever the soul was moved to such expression. While such praises might flow abundantly at times, too often the soul underwent periods of dryness, when, if left to its own, it would give over its religious duty. To compensate for these periods, Taylor set himself the task of regular meditation; he forced himself to sing the Lord's praises even when he would have preferred not to.

These were the periods when Christ's praises were wrung from his Muse with great effort—when he could only sing lamentations and not anthems: "But duty raps upon her door for verse. / That makes her bleed a poem through her searce" (PM, 2.30). Even when it would be preferable to be still, Taylor wrote "But thus I force myself to speak of thee" (PM, 2.132); and it seems clear that many of his meditations were the forced product of this sense of duty.

Throughout forty-four years he complains over and over again that his imagination is at fault, that he cannot invent new ways of giving the subject of his meditations poetic body. He would have agreed with Thomas H. Johnson's criticism that the meditations are repetitious both in their ideas and their images and that they are not, as a whole, impressively inventive.[11] Taylor actually made the same criticism of them—and did it as he wrote—for he knew that these acts of devotion had to be written even when his imagination or "phansy," as he usually refers to it, refused to work:

> My phansy's in a maze, my thoughts aghast,
>   Words in an ecstasy; my tell-tale tongue
> Is tongue-tied, and my lips are padlocked fast
>   To see thy kingly glory in to throng.
>   I can, yet cannot tell this glory just,
>   In silence bury't must not, yet I must.
>
> (PM, 1.17)

His "phansy" was too often befogged and dark, coarse, shattered, puzzled, unspun, chilly, benumbed, tattered, rusty; in his seventies he confessed: "My muse's hermitage is grown so old" (PM, 2.122). Partly by virtue of a darkened reason incapable of conceiving Christ's transcendent glories and partly because he composed poetry when his "phansy" was not up to the task, he wrote poorly and he knew it.

Although part of a calculated strategy of failure, the apologetic openings of a sixth of his meditations are also an index to his poetic limitations. The one characteristic about his poems that bothered him most frequently is their roughness or harshness. At one level this concern is merely a sense of inelegance in comparison to the beauty he desired to express. That is, Taylor sees Christ as the great hero of his poems, and so describes his poetry as attempting "t'run on heroic golden feet" (*PM*, 1.21). He promises Christ, "I'll sing / And make thy praise on my heroics run"; but too often he could only limp. Occasionally his poetry excited him, but at other times the impossibility of his task and his own spiritual coldness prevented his writing well. Attempts to force poetry in such states of dullness merely "wrack my rhymes to pieces" (*PM*, 1.10). He calls his rhymes ragged, and says his voice is rough, his tongue blunt (*PM*, 1.23). Everything he writes, it seems to him at times, he fouls with his pen's "harsh jar" (*PM*, 2.138).

Taylor's roughness or harshness, then, is not, like Donne's, an intentional departure from the fluidity of Spenser's lines for the sake of dramatic, or at least conversational, reality. Taylor's roughness he judges and perhaps means to be taken as a fault, which he modestly blames on his own lack of ability: "I would do well, but have too little skill," he moans, offering his poetic devotions as poor and unworthy products, though the best at his disposal. "Homely" is the word modern critics have been pleased to accept from Taylor as descriptive of his style (*PM*, 2.141). Insofar as they see Taylor as a perfunctory rhymer, a writer of harsh lines, as difficult of pronunciation, or as fatally attracted to hackneyed diction or the dull repetition of stock metaphors, they seem to become complicit in Taylor's own self-appraisal and self-blame. In fact, Taylor goes further than most critics in rejecting some of his rhymes, which he thinks "would choke the air with stinks" (*PM*, 2.67B).

But his shame about his poor, dull notes—as he calls them—and with his leaden metaphors of ragged nonsense, clumsy lines, feeble words, and awkward rhymes springs finally from comparison of his own work with the most beautiful of all pictures of Christ's glory—the Gospels. He sees his own poetry as a gloss upon the poetry of the Lord: "Thy Spirit's pencil hath thy glory told, / And I do stut, commenting on the same" (*PM*, 2.123B). By comparison with the inspired writing of the Bible Taylor sees, therefore, his own work as poor. For this reason he turns to the scriptures for texts and doctrines, hoping thereby to warm his benumbed "phansy," and to free his stubborn pen. The one thing that Gospel language has for Taylor is power—the power to move admiration, love, gratidude, all the affections; and the force to reframe the human heart, to make it congruent with God's will. Taylor also

associates total power with beauty, for he reasons that a thing that is
all-powerful can admit no defect or want and, therefore, must have a
mighty and transcendent beauty (C, 212–13). Taylor does not develop
this notion of beauty himself, but it seems to lie behind much of his
self-criticism and to add an aesthetic dimension to judgments that seem
not to be concerned directly with the idea of beauty. The one word that
he attaches most frequently to both his diction and his inventive ability
is "feeble," which carries for him not only the meaning of weakness and
powerlessness but, for that very reason, lack of beauty.

Thus through weakness of imagination and reason he finds himself
capable of doing no more in his attempt to beautify Christ than to
dirty, smut, and darken that most powerful of all beauties. Only
through true and saving faith can the poet hope to write truly beautiful
poetry. Saving faith is basic to all activity—physical, mental, even
spiritual. It is the oil that permits the workings of grace to move
smoothly; without it, all speech, even preaching, is like the chattering
of magpies. So Taylor's constant petition to have his candle lighted
with Christ's illuminating grace; his mirror shined; his mental eye
annointed with saving salve; his seed impregnated; and his reason, will,
and understanding rectified—all this is a plea to be made a poet fit to
sing heroics in praise of the Lord.

Chapter Four

Accomplishment

The Nondevotional Poems

Edward Taylor did not discover his major poetic enterprise as a devotional poet until his forties, although he had been a versifier since his English school days. Indeed the devotional poems constitute only a quarter of his verse. Except for a handful of short lyrics, the bulk of this work is social, occasional, political, historical, and essentially public. There are greetings to friends, a marriage proposal, the massive metrical history of Christianity, scurrilous and obsessive retellings of the infamous female pope of the Middle Ages, a college declamation, satirical debates, and a small number of funeral elegies. Produced in the great satirical age of Dryden, Taylor's public poems are for the most part a tribute to ideological zeal—tactless, tasteless, and talentless.

They show a young man with a penchant for baroque grotesqueries, an affection for acrostics, anagrams, and chronograms, a sophomoric delight in ingenious amphibologies (the full force of puns being hardly available to writers before the age of dictionaries), and a tolerance for doggerel that would stagger a goat. Dryden, and later Addison and Pope, were busily weaning British poetry away from these devices of "false wit," but we must remember that in 1692 the poems of the Mexican nun, Sor Juana de la Cruz, "la decima musa," were published to great applause in Spain, though full of the Gongoresque affectations that Taylor's rustic baroque seems to parody.

One subject, one theme, one experience transcended the artificialities of Taylor's early verse—death—the death of prominent social pillars, the death of his children and of his wife. As a personal inevitability, death offered no poetic difficulty to Taylor, whose two versions of "A Fig For Thee, Oh Death!" recall the arrogance of Donne's much more successful "Death, Be Not Proud!" But with public figures, the issue was more complex as well as more engaging. Deaths in the 1660s and 1670s marked the end of a generation of colonial heroes, a crumbling of the battlements of true religion in the New World. They were reminders that the mere scorning of death was not enough. The verse elegy sought not only to memorialize the dead—a verbal equivalent to the carved gravestone markers so brilliantly portrayed in Allan I. Ludwig's *Graven Images*[1]—but also to close social ranks and to carry out the principles for which the deceased stood.

To effect this transfer, New England elegists, whether adopting other features of the classical elegy or not, frequently introduced the feature of the dead speaking to the living, and of the transformation of the dead's name through anagrams and acrostics into living truths. This transfer of names in the interest of cultural continuity strangely parallels the Iroquois condolence ritual—also a seventeenth-century phenomenon—whereby a name like Hiawatha is handed down through generations, ensuring identity through change. That New England culture might have shared both values and techniques with the skulking rascals responsible for King Philip's War would surely have appeared obnoxious, if not incredible, to Puritans of Taylor's generation. That, however, does not rule out the possibility of influence.[2]

The point, nonetheless, is that Taylor approached the elegy from a position of very high awareness of social significance, and that in his best poem of this sort—the elegy for Samuel Hooker—he more than equalled the best produced by John Wilson, John Fiske, or Benjamin Tompson. Hooker's death in 1697 becomes an occasion to preach a verse Jeremiad against apostasy in New England. Hooker himself is merely a point of focus, a chance for Taylor to declare his deepest ecclesiastical concerns, an eminence from which he can descry and rout the enemies of Congregationalism. Because it is at once an elegy and a public edict, it shows Taylor at his public best.

In the opening section, after a conventional statement of grief. Taylor mentions Hooker's death briefly and then introduces the main issue. Taylor is less concerned with Samuel Hooker himself than with his "choice name," for Samuel was the son of Thomas Hooker, the famed founder of the Hartford colony.[3] Now that this brave Jonathan is dead, Taylor asks, will no David arise to avenge him? These are times

> When birds new hatcht wear, as in nest they lie,
> Presbytick down, pinfeathered prelacy
> (Young cockerils, whose combs soar up like spires,
> That force their dams, and crow against their sires).

Where, he inquires, apparently addressing all of New England,

> Where hast thou left thy strength and potency?
> And Congregational artillery?
> We need the same and need it more and more.
> For Babel's cannons 'gainst our bulwarks roar.

Just as his concern for the problem of apostasy had appeared most directly in his preaching about the Lord's Supper in 1693 and 1694, so here again he aims at the Presbyterian sentiments of Solomon Stoddard. By the year of Hooker's death the direction in which New England was wavering had become quite clear.

The second movement of the dirge is directed "To New England," and begins, "Alas! Alas! New England, go weep. / Thy loss is great in him." It then engraves a character of a good Puritan preacher, with Hooker as the model. Taylor describes his wisdom, inventiveness, and excellent rhetoric; his habit of creating witty maxims; and his strength and sturdiness in carrying out God's will, whether as peacemaker or as corrosive rebuker. The one quality to emerge most visibly from this category of traits is his steadiness; because of it, Taylor implies, New England would do well to emulate him. This is the main lesson of the poem, and the remarks he makes about Hooker as a rich divine, a preacher never "notion sick," and a pious father and husband move quickly to Hooker's death. At this point Taylor raises the main question—"But art thou gone, brave Hooker, hence? and why?" His answer to his own question seems to be that "the country's sins" brought Hooker's death to pass, and hereupon he turns to diagnose the ills of New England, whose brains are giddied by false preachers and false Gospel. The terseness of his prognosis—"Such symptoms say, if nothing else will ease, / Thy sickness soon wil cure thy sad disease"— speaks no good for New England. If it continues to decline, Taylor indicates where it must end:

> Apostasy, wherewith thou art thus driven
> Unto the tents of Presbyterianism
> (Which is refined Prelacy at best),
> Will not stay long here in her tents, and rest,
> But o'er this bridge will carry thee apace
> Into the realm of Prelate's arch, the place
> Where open sinners, vile, unmasked indeed,
> Are welcome guests (if they can say the Creed)
> Unto Christ's table, while they can their sins
> Atone in courts by offering silverlings.

Only one cure can save the country, and that Taylor prescribes: "Watch, watch thou then: reform thy life: refine / Thyself from thy declensions. Tend thy line."

In part 3, "To Connecticut," Taylor reminds the colony of its "Foundation Stone," the elder Hooker; and he asserts that now no one is left to help the colony recover from its ills. And in part 4 he turns to Farmington, the town where Hooker presided as minister; in a series of paradoxes, he calls her to lament:

> Alas, poor Farmington, of all the rest
> Most happy and unhappy, blesst, unblesst:
> Most happy having such an happiness:
> And most unhappy losing of no less.

At this point Taylor uses Hooker's death as a prophecy both made and fulfilled by the Farmington minister—as an exemplum of Farmington's and all New England's dire prospects. Hooker had preached, five days before he died, on a text from Jer. 6:26, which Taylor very skillfully metaphrases:

> Oh! Daughter of my people, (that last text)
> Gird thee with sackcloth, wallow thee perplext
> In ashes. Mourn thou lamentably
> As for an only son: weep bitterly,
> For lo, the Spoiler suddenly shall come
> Upon us.

Then he recalls for Farmington that "the prophesy / Had an accomplishment before your eye," for, resting while they sang a Psalm, Hooker blessed them and collapsed. The Spoiler had come, and Taylor draws the moral clearly: "Lord, grant it ben't an omen of our fate, / Foreshewing our apostate-following state." Again he prescribes the bitter purgation:

> Search into thy sin,
> Repent and grieve that ere thou grievedst him,
> Or rather God in him, lest suddenly
> The Spoiler still should on thee come and stroy.

What if they reject the pill and refuse the physic? "Shall angling cease? And no more fish be took, / That thou callst home thy Hooker with his hook?" With this comparatively dignified pun Taylor ends part 4. The final section, "To the Family Relict," which addresses Samuel Hooker's widow and children, contains the finest touches of Taylor's artistry. For what consolation it may offer, Taylor personifies New England in assuring the widow's "Poor bleeding soul" that "New England lays her head / To thine, to weep with thee over thy dead." He then most adroitly manipulates his consolation so as to have the departed Hooker speak to his wife from bliss:

> Christ's napkin take, grace's green taffity,
> And wipe therewith thy weeping, wat'ry eye,
> And thou shalt see thy Hooker all o'er gay
> With Christ in bliss, adorn'd with glory's ray,
> And putting out his shining hand to thee,
> Saying, "My Honey, mourn no more for me."

When Hooker's speech is ended, Taylor turns to the children to urge them to accept the spirit of their father and grandfather and to admonish them not to be like some ungrateful offspring who pull out their father's brains, make wassail bowls of their skulls, and stuff their eyes with folly. The great name of Hooker must endure no apostasy; for the dead Samuel was a cabinet of virtue and a treasury of grace; a bright temple of piety in print; and a stage of war, a golden pulpit, and an oratory of prayer. He compounds this list of conventional metaphors, takes leave of the body, and adds a feeble cliché as epitaph to the whole.

This commemoration of Samuel Hooker is Taylor's finest elegy, and it is also one of the finest in the New England metaphysical style.[4] It is, therefore, an excellent representative of all the devices of the elegy, except for classical allusion, which Taylor prefers to avoid. It also represents the summation and refinement of his abilities in the form— puns and biblical allusion; the speech of the deceased and the exemplum; the personification of country, colony, and town; the carefully inwrought text from Jeremiah to support his own Jeremiad; and the fully accomplished organization of the whole.

Taylor's elegies of a quarter-century earlier—on Zechariah Symmes, Francis Willoughby, John Allen, and President Charles Chauncy of Harvard—are elaborately ingenious, but not personally involved, as is the Hooker poem. One suspects that after the intervening experience of personal loss himself—the deaths of five children and his first wife Elizabeth—he became conscious at a deeper level of the personal losses involved. That is to some extent evident in the elegy on his wife written in 1689.

Fifteen years earlier, in the most playful mood he ever allowed to show in writing, he courted Miss Fitch of Norwich in an elaborate poem accompanied by a very brief mock sermon. The poem runs the entire alphabet down the left margin as the first letters of each line, implying that the entire English language is implicit in his plea and his promises. This is certainly his most quaint and complicated form, for the lines are arranged so that within the general acrostic two figures are described—a ring inside a triangle, tangential with the triangle at three points. By carefully placing the lines of his alphabet acrostic, Taylor allows certain letters to fall along the triangle; read separately, these letters yield the message: "The ring of love my pleasant heart must be, Truely confin'd within the trinity." The ring within the triangle uses the same letters at points of tangent, spelling out, "Love's ring I send, that hath no end."[5]

Now in 1689 with the object of his playful courtship dead, Taylor remembers the early word game.[6] In the elegy, he imagines Elizabeth speaking to him from beyond the grave, chiding him for singing: "My dear, dear love, reflect thou no such thing, / Will grief permit you at my grave to sing?" He agrees that songs and sorrows may not belong together, but compares his dirge to the groans that grief wrings from his heart. Moreover, having begun in song, it is appropriate their marriage should end the same way.

> What, shall my preface to our true love knot
> Frisk in acrostic rhyme? And may I not
> Now at our parting, with poetic knocks
> Break a salt tear to pieces as it drops?
> Did David's bitter sorrow at the dusts
> Of Jonathan raise such poetic gusts?
> Do emperors interr'd in verses lie?
> And mayn't such feet run from my weeping eye?
> Nay, duty lies upon me much; and shall
> I in thy coffin nail thy virtues all?
> How shall thy babes, and theirs, thy virtuous shine
> Know or pursue unless I them define?

Out of this combination of motives—to preserve her memory, to instruct his children and grandchildren, to release his grief by giving it voice, and to raise for her a monument of neither marble nor stone, but of powerful and immortalizing rhyme—he approaches logically the third section. The connection between parts is, therefore, closer than in the other elegies.

Resolved not to abuse Elizabeth's modesty by hyperbole, Taylor described her generally as he considers her various rôles in life—child, neighbor, mistress of her household, mother, wife, and finally Christian and church member. Some details are specific—the fact that her mother was dead, that she had experienced conversion at home, that she enjoyed Michael Wigglesworth's *Day of Doom,* and that she reconciled herself to misfortune with the words, "An all-wise God doth this"—but the virtues displayed are obedience, tenderness, meekness, courtesy, compassion, prudence, dutifulness, humility, modesty, patience, and piety. In short, Taylor draws an idealized portrait of the Puritan wife—one to be emulated rather than known. Lacking figure and illustration, the poem mourns moderately; it is a very self-conscious and restrained performance, which is not without tenderness and warmth on Taylor's part, but which was designed for the eyes of others, and so expressed love and loss discreetly.

Much more personal, less discreet, and ironically the most public of Taylor's poems (three stanzas were published in Cotton Mather's *Right Thoughts in Sad Hours,* London, 1689) is his fine "Upon Wedlock, and Death of Children," composed sometime after the August death of his daughter Abigail in 1682.[7] Although formal elegies often were composed to commemorate the death of infants, this is not such an elegy, but a general reflection on one of the griefs of marriage. It was during Abigail's sickness that Taylor committed himself to the series of devotional poems on which his fame rests, dating the first meditation on 25 July 1682. Like the meditations, "Upon Wedlock" rejects decasyllabic couplets in favor of stanzas made up of pentameter lines rhymed *ababcc.* The stanza provides units of thought and image that structure his expression much more rigidly than elegiac did. The effect is an almost classical restraint, much like Ben Jonson's, against which the personal anguish of the experience Taylor describes creates a tension he rarely matches. The sense of strain and tension produces a powerful statement, but it is controlled by the strength of the poet's religious faith and by his compliance with God's demanding will.

In this attitude Taylor steps midway between Donne and Herbert. Donne, who solves his spiritual conflicts by fiat, leaves one feeling that the solution provided has not actually resolved the question in his soul. Herbert echoes Donne's struggles vociferously, as in "Love" and "The

Collar"; but, when he submits to God's will at the end of the poem, we realize that the sound and the fury have been merely a rhetorical device to accentuate the final, child-like submission. In "Upon Wedlock, and Death of Children," Taylor submits to the Lord's will as fully as Herbert; but Taylor's struggle, while not so loud in expostulation as Donne's, is no mere rhetorical or intellectual quibble but an intensely personal and human one.

The poem opens easily and prettily. God ties a curious knot in paradise. The knot, a true-love's knot, a wedding knot, suggests a plot of flowers; and it occasions flower, slip, plant, sprout, seed, and perfume imagery throughout the rest of the poem. He compares the knot to that of Gordius which the baffled Alexander the Great could untie only with his sword. But "No Alexander's sword can it divide," he says. The sword allusion forms the only image contrary to the prettiness of the knot of flowers, though it occurs only to be dismissed. Flowers planted in this knot grow "gay and glorious," continues Taylor, "Unless an hellish breath do singe their plumes." Like the sword of the first stanza, this is the only image which contrasts with the flowers; and it represents, of course, sin and death. With Elizabethan taste he continues to describe the knot:

> Here primrose, cowslips, roses, lillies blow,
>   With violets and pinks that void perfumes,
> Whose beauteous leaves o'er laid with honey-dew,
>   And chanting birds cherp out sweet music true.

In the third stanza Taylor relates himself to the marriage knot: "When in this knot I planted was, my stock / Soon knotted, and a manly flower out brake." He refers to his first-born, Samuel; and, in the next line a second child, his daughter Elizabeth is born: "And after it my branch again did knot, / Brought out another flower, its sweet-breathed mate." Still the images are pleasant, the two flowers smiling, sweet, and perfumed. Besides the natural meaning of perfume as the fragrance of flowers, the term usually means for Taylor some kind of satisfaction. The most frequent use of perfume in his poetry is as a pillar of incense rising to please the Lord, and it is a familiar metaphor for prayer. It probably represents in this poem the satisfaction the children bring him. There is no utterly contrary image in this stanza, but the word *knot* takes on a sense inherent in it from the beginning, but not emphasized—a sense of hardness and tightness, stress, and effort, consistent with the strain of childbirth.

Elizabeth died almost exactly a year after her birth, apparently quickly and suddenly, in an "unlookt for, dolesome, darksome hour." The "glorious hand from glory" that cropped this flower "almost tore the root up of the same," he confesses, recalling the sword of the first stanza, in the word "crop." Yet, in this stanza the images are not all dark; and, though nearly uprooted himself, Taylor consoles himself with the knowledge that his daughter is attended to heaven by angels. In fact, he reconciles his loss stoically in the next stanza: he offers his child to Christ as a pledge or assurance that he will follow, as a sacrifice of part of himself.

> But pausing on't, this sweet perfum'd my thought,
>   Christ would in glory have a flower, choice, prime,
> And having choice, chose this my branch forth brought.
>   Lord, take't. I thank thee, thou tak'st ought of mine.

Thus reconciled, he has another child, a boy again, and in 1681 "another sweet," a daughter Abigail. Again, almost a year after her birth, "The former hand" took her away. But this time the child's death was not an easy one, and his consolation came only with tremendous effort: "But oh! the tortures, vomit, screechings, groans, / And six weeks' fever would pierce hearts like stones." Unlike Taylor's imagined golden door of death swinging easily to let the dead swim through, Abigail's passage is a bramble of undecorated, unvarnished vomit, groans, and fever.

This time, when Taylor submits to God's will, his submission is not so witty. He does not even try to invent a new figure to express it, and the last stanza echoes none of the self-satisfied thanks of the fifth stanza.

> Grief o'er doth flow: and nature fault would find,
>   Were not thy will my spell, charm, joy, and gem,
> That as I said, I say, take, Lord, they're thine.
>   I piecemeal pass to glory bright in them.
>   I joy, may I sweet flowers for glory breed,
>   Whether thou getst them green, or lets them seed.

Reconciliation to grief through obedience to God's will is attained with joy, but a clouded joy. Unlike Taylor's *Meditations,* this last stanza has no dizzying rhetoric. Not sullen, yet it does not sing. And we are aware that Taylor has learned Job's lesson: he is not to speak from the bitterness of his heart.

"Upon Wedlock, and Death of Children" belongs among Taylor's finest accomplishments. Among them it stands unique; for it is the only poem prompted by no specific occasion as were the elegies, by no sense of regular duty like the *Meditations,* and by no literary motive like *God's Determinations.* The "I" of the poem is not the representative soul or the church as it so often seems to be in the larger poems; it speaks for Edward Taylor, frontier minister and physician who has lost two children and who seeks relief from his sorrow in poetry. The intense personal involvement and the universality of his problem elevate the poem from among his elegiac verse. The poet-physician touches the open wound in his spirit with a salty finger, but only to apply a healing balm.

Preparatory Meditations

Precisely why Taylor began writing and collecting his *Preparatory Meditations* in 1682 is a moot question, but his growing concern for the Congregational way may have had something to do with it. In his illuminating study of "the Transfiguration of Eucharist Symbols in Seventeenth Century English Poetry," Professor Malcolm Mackenzie Ross suggests most broadly that disenchantment with the actualities of state and church in Herbert, Crashaw, Vaughan, and Milton largely propelled them to the creation of new—and different—worlds into which they retreated poetically.[8] Something of this reaction may lurk behind Taylor's poetic mysticism, but his preaching and controversies after he began the meditations argue no surrender of the New England vision.

Two American publications of 1682 may have offered both encouragement and precedent for Taylor's poems. One, Increase Mather's *Practical Truths Tending to Promote Godliness,*[9] urged meditation as a means of attaining a transforming, mystical vision of the Lord; and it also emphasized that a sense of duty should accompany the exercise. The other was the third printing of a book of *Daily Meditations* by a young seaman named Philip Pain.[10] Although Pain's amateurish attempts at a stanza similar to Taylor's frequently echo the sentiments and manner of George Herbert, Pain's main concern, unlike Taylor's, was entirely with the imminence of death and with the transitoriness of all earthly things. From Loyola to Cotton Mather the injunction to the reader to imagine himself at the point of death to increase the immediacy and urgency of the act of devotion was traditional. Furthermore, Pain's six-line stanza is merely a grouping of three couplets.

Although the specific reason for Taylor's *Meditations* remains entirely unknown, there is little question about Professor Martz's judgment that "Taylor's standing as a poet must be measured by a full and careful reading of the *Meditations*."[11] Much of what I have said about Taylor depends upon the *Meditations* seen as a whole, but I have so far approached them only thematically.

Considered formally, they appear more similar than dissimilar. While tracing the elements of uniformity—as Martz has done—is a very valuable way to come to a total appraisal, it tends to neglect the variations within the *Meditations* as a whole; a look, therefore, at the different things Taylor undertakes in the poems and at the different characteristics they possess may also be illuminating. First, there is uniformity, for all the poems use the same versatile stanzaic form: iambic pentameter lines rhyming *ababcc*. Occasionally Taylor allows his thought, image, and syntax to run from one stanza to the next; but, usually, the six-line unit marks the structural limit of his statement. This structural limitation gives a regularity to the cadence of his verse beyond that imposed by the decasyllabics themselves, and it also provides a kind of angularity and steadiness to the development of both thoughts and images. Against this formal regularity, Taylor's roughness—sometimes intentional, usually not—is even more striking than it would be in a freer form.

The main disadvantage of the stanzaic method lies in its limitations for a long poem, where it inhibits dramatic changes of pace; interrupts development; and, for want of emphasis, slips too easily into tediousness. This monotony is especially evident in Meditation 2.58, the longest and one of the dullest of the poems, though length alone is not responsible. The shortest poems, like Meditation 1.1, on the other hand, breed no weariness; its three stanzas are, in fact, most inconspicuous; and the brevity emphasizes rather than impairs the unity of the whole poem. At least for Taylor, then, the form works most successfully when restricted to fewer than ten stanzas; and this he seems to have realized, for most of his *Meditations* fall within this limit.

The structure of each of the poems is likewise similar. They begin with a question—"My Blessed Lord, art thou a lily flower?" or "Am I thy gold? or purse, Lord, for thy wealth?"—or a statement of fact, which usually, like the question, presents a metaphor: "My silver chest a spark of love up locks," or "Like to the marigold, I blushing close," or some exclamation. The exclamation is usually a series of epithets—"Oh! leaden heel'd," "Oh! golden rose," "A crown of glory, Oh!" "My Lord, my life, can envy ever be," "Oh! wealthy theme! Oh! feeble," "A king, a king, a king indeed, a king." Sometimes it functions as the opening of a longer sentence: "Raptures of love, surprising loveliness / That burst through heavens all, in rapid flashes." Occasionally it is self-admonishing: "Astonished stand, my Soul: why dost thou start," or "My sin! my sin, my God, these cursed dregs." These opening lines, or the remainder of the stanzas they open, set the subject of the meditation.

From this point, the poems develop the opening idea or image. Usually Taylor develops the idea or the underlying logic rather than the image itself, but there are some notable exceptions. As a result of this concentration upon ideas, however, there is very little to be said about the central development of the poems, where diversity predominates. As Stanford points out, Taylor's development is at times grossly inconsistent. Meditation 1.20, for example, begins with Christ's soaring to heaven swifter than angels. The second stanza shows him seated in "His bright sedan," an azure cloud that acts as his chariot. Stanza 3 denies the chariot image and insists Christ rises by the rungs of Jacob's Ladder. But by the end of that stanza the ladder image is altered to one of "golden stepping stones" to the throne of Deity.

If the second part of the poems is diverse—sometimes reduced to a single stanza, sometimes developed through several—the final part is uniformly the same. These *Meditations* are a form, we must remember, of secret prayer; and prayer combines both praise and petition. The logic of the poems is designed to bring the poet to the final stanza of petition, which ordinarily applies the consideration of the preceding two parts of the poem to his own condition; usually this stanza combines the personal application with his personal request: "Lord, make my soul thy plate; thine image bright / Within the circle of the same enfoil"; "Pare off, my Lord, from me, I pray, my pelf"; "Lord, make me to the Pentecost repair, / Make me thy guest too at this feast." It ends with the promise to praise and give thanks if the petition is granted: "Yet thy rich grace save me from sin and death? / And I will tune thy praise with holy breath"; "I'll sing / And make thy praise on my heroics ring."

This threefold pattern governs all the *Meditations,* and it tends to make each poem a discrete unit—an entirely separate effort, structurally, from the others, yet one exactly like them. I think this tendency argues against Martz's suggestion that "the *Meditations* are written in sequences, sometimes with tight links between the poems."[12] The linking is certainly there, but the sequence is quite accidental. Meditation 1.3, for example, is built up primarily from images of odors, and the last stanza petitions: "My spirits let with thy perfume be fed / And make thy odors, Lord, my nostrils fare." The following poem, "The Experience," begins as if it remembered the preceding experience: "Oh! that I always breath'd in such an air / As I suck't in, feeding on sweet content." Meditation 1.4, which centers upon the Rose of Sharon image, is followed by "The Reflexion," which opens with the same image in the first two stanzas.

In the second series, Meditation 2.20 ends with the lines "And I will, as I walk herein, / Thy glory thee in temple music bring." The first line of the following meditation is "Rich temple! Fair! Rich festivals, my Lord." Meditation 58 petitions the Lord in the third stanza:

> Christen mine eyeballs with thine eye-salve then,
> Mine eyes will spy how Isra'l's journeying
> Into, and out of Egypt's bondage den,
> A glass thy visage was imbellisht in.

The eye-mirror image does not recur in the following eighteen stanzas, but in the opening of Meditation 59 it is the basis of the first stanza:

> Wilt thou enoculate within mine eye
> Thy image bright, my Lord, that bright doth shine
> Forth in the cloudy-fiery pillar high,
> Thy tabernacle's looking-glass divine?
> What glorious rooms are then mine eyeholes made,
> Thine image on my window's glass portray'd?

And in Meditation 2.60A again the scriptures are described as "a shining glass, wherein thy face, / My Lord, as bread of life, is clearly seen." Immediately following is a meditation that again, though very incidentally, uses eye-imagery; it concludes with the lament, "I'm sick." Meditation 2.61 introduces Christ as a healer, and Meditation 2.62 presents him with the herbs and remedies to supply his "doctor's shop." The herbs of purification come from a garden, which contributes centrally to the images of the next three meditations. Such a cluster of related and interlocking images serves to unite eight poems; and similar clusters in other poems seem to add support to Martz's suggestion. But in refutation of Martz's suggestion, Taylor himself has pointed out that the poems are chiefly upon the doctrines he preached, and it was still popular in this period to prepare a plan for sermons—as in his *Christographia* ones—and to carry the plan through for three years or more. Babette Levy indicates that often the Puritan preacher "lingered on a favorite or meaty passage, as John Warham did for twenty-seven sermons on Rom. 1:5. With equal fervor of spirit, Thomas Hooker spent nearly a year on Acts 2:37, and Thomas Shepard, after four years on Matt. 25:1–13, congratulated himself that he had not, after the fashion of Papist commentators, squeezed the last bit of meaning out of it."[13] Taylor's Meditations 2.115–153, which cite texts from Cant. 5:10 to 7:6, cover a span of six years. Because they were based upon his sermons, we know that he must have been preaching a series of sermons based on Canticles over the same length of time. Whether in the case of these poems, or in the twenty-odd poems on typology that begin the second series, or the interlocking images, or the image clusters, each of the poems is separately conceived and developed. Their sequential relationship is an accident of the sermon sequence, and not a poetic intention, though certainly Martz is right in concluding that individual poems gain in strength and richness, and are, in a very real way, sustained by the sequence in which they occur.[14]

Because the motive and the general subject of the poems are uniform, their attitude and tone never vary; and they support the structural uniformity of the *Meditations.* Unlike Herbert's *Temple* or Traherne's *Poems of Felicity,* Taylor played very little with verse technique within the general structure. Why he avoided such experiments is not clear, but his avoidance is regrettable; for, when he does experiment a few times, the results are excellent. In "The Return," for example, he converts the couplet at the end of each stanza into a refrain, with minor incremental changes to fit the refrain to the thought of each stanza. Meditation 1.16 resorts to a device used successfully by Sir Thomas Wyatt in "Disdain Me Not" and by Spenser in his first *Amoretti* sonnet. Spenser opens his first quatrain with "Happy ye leaves," the second with "And happy lines," the third with "And happy rymes"; all three terms are then summed up in the first line of the concluding couplet: "Leaves, lines, and rymes, seeke her to please alone." Taylor's second stanza begins:

> I cannot see, nor will thy will aright.
> Nor see to wail my woe, my loss and hew
> Nor all the shine in all the sun can light
> My candle, nor its heat my heart renew.

The next line sums up these terms: "See, wail, and will thy will I must, or must / From heaven's sweet shine to hell's hot flame be thrust." This is the only occasion when he tries such a technique. Rarely he turns to some form of refrain, as he does most successfully in Meditation 1.40, where he seems to echo Herbert's "Was ever grief like mine?" in "The Sacrifice." But in Taylor's eleven stanzas the question is put only five times, and he varies its position in the stanza and in the line very effectively. Only one other time does he use a refrain-like device, which is structurally reminiscent of many of Wyatt's lyrics, but ideologically most like Donne's "A Hymne to God the Father" with its punning refrain on his own name: "When thou hast done, thou hast not done, / For, I have more." In Meditation 2.95, stanzas 5, 6, and 7 begin with "But that's not all"; and the seventh concludes the series with these last words:

> *But that's not all.* Leaving these doleful rooms
>   Thou com'st and tak'st them by the hand, most high,
> Dost them translate out from their death bed tombs,
>   To th'rooms prepar'd, fill'd with eternal joy.
>   Them crown'st and thron'st there, there their lips be shall
>   Pearld with eternal praises, *that's but all.*

But the refrain is not a major device in the poem. It is rather absorbed into the total structure, where it perhaps functions more subtly than Donne's, but not so effectively.

For variety within the total structure, Taylor preferred less obvious devices of rhyme, meter, and repetition. A list of Taylor's rhymes turns up some unexpected combinations, brought about by a variety of rhyming tricks. The surprise is that he rarely rhymes multisyllabic words; there are, therefore, few feminine rhymes and no double or triple rhymes. Limiting himself to stressed monosyllables, he turns frequently to forms of off or slant rhyme to increase the number of words from which he can choose. Often identical vowel sounds satisfy his ear, regardless of their accompanying consonants: *sweet / reech; keep / sweet; breathes / leaves; like / light.* Identical vowels plus *r* and different terminal

consonants also satisfy him: *heart/spark; curb/spur'd.* And often the
final *r* is enough alone to constitute a rhyme: *where/here; restore/cure;
flower/pour. Clear* can therefore by rhymed with *ere, there,* and *were.*
Occasionally the terminal consonant, especially a stopped consonant,
makes the rhyme: *bread/had; broad/God; deckt/fret.*

He exercises greater license with nasals, terminal *g,* and terminal *s.*
In the first place, he apparently makes no distinction between the
terminal nasals themselves: *slime/chalybdine; in/him; resume/tune; grain
/same.* When he combines the nasal with another consonant, he still
seems to make no distinction, though what happens when that extra
consonant is *g* is not clear; *shine/climb; strong/hung; rank/cramp.* It
seems at times that Professor Warren's conclusion that "he did not
sound terminal *g*"[15] is born out—*bin/spring; thing/brim*—but it is
doubtful that Taylor ignored the final *g* at other times, as in *tongue/
throng; run/tongue; king/fling;* he seems, in fact, to sound it or not as
the situation demands. This last combination exemplifies the freedom
he gains through the terminal *s,* which, whether for plurality or possession, he adds freely to rhymes such as *should/folds; stand/hands; doors/
o'er.* He also rhymes voiced and unvoiced *s*—*lies/sacrifice; pass/was; is/
this*—and matches the unvoiced *s* freely with *sh* as in *afresh/deliciousness;
this/dish.* Sometimes the voiced *s* alone is adequate for the rhyme as in
seas/rays. The *th* and *f* are also frequent: *goeth/loaf; wealth/self.*

Other rhymes, slightly unusual, are commonplace in his verse:
*confin'd/conjoyn'd, choice/price; would/cold; word/hoard; wave/have;
convays/says; key/day;* the words *to* and *do* rhyme with *flow, below,* and
know. Ordinarily Taylor drops the *-ed* ending on adjectives and past
tenses, but sometimes he maintains them solely for the sake of rhyme as
in these cases: *polishèd/head; lessenèd/fed.* In the case of multisyllabic
words, this often wrenches the natural meter to allow the final stress to
fall on the rhymed syllable: Taylor can thus rhyme *jar* with *scribener*
once and again with *pottinger.* On the other hand, instead of lengthening words by that third syllable, he frequently cuts a two- or three-
syllable word down or combines two words into one by elision: *in it*
becomes *in't* to rhyme with *ink, o'er* for *over* rhymes with *doors;* and
drown us becomes *drounds* to rhyme with *ground.* As outrageous and
artificial as the devices are, one rarely feels that Taylor has turned to
them in desperation. They seem rather a natural means for him to
increase his rhyming vocabulary, and he often uses them so well that
they are unobtrusively absorbed into the stanza. Unlike Emily Dickinson, whose slant and off rhymes are intended to catch, startle, and

please the reader by their effects, Taylor's seem intended to disappear into the folds of the stanzaic pattern.

Taylor's extending and truncating words for the sake of rhyme inevitably results in some roughness and often an excellent compactness as these tricks impinge on the metrics of the verse: lines like "To th'rooms prepar'd, fill'd with eternal joy. / Them crown'st and thron'st there, there their lips be shall," are impossibly bad; and the last part sounds like an echo of the worst of the *Bay Psalm Book*. Usually Taylor does better than this, and his roughness becomes part of his idiom rather than the accidental aftermath of an unsuccessful struggle to squeeze a thought into ten syllables. Since the roughness is characteristic, the means by which he secures it are easily analyzed.

In his elegy about Hooker, Taylor points out that under the force of emotion, a man does not speak easily, fluently, smoothly, but stutters, "Cutting off sentences by enterjections / Made by the force of hard beset affections" (11.3–4). In his sermons he exhorts his listeners to let their affections be moved, and in the poems he tries to utter his praise already beset by his own moved affections. Therefore, he cuts off his sentence and interjects exclamations, parenthetical phrases or clauses, and appositions. The result is a line broken into two, three, and sometimes even more parts. Meditation 1.1, as a case in point, ends with a stanza made up of half lines rather than whole ones:

> Oh! that thy love might overflow my heart!
> To fire the same with love: for love I would.
> But! oh! my streight'ned breast! my lifeless spark!
> My fireless flame! What! chilly love and cold?
> In measure small! In manner chilly! See.
> Lord, blow the coal: thy love enflame in me.

Not a single line reads smoothly, and four of them are broken by two pauses. In this instance, each line is also end-stopped, accentuating the brevity of the phrases. The three parallel phrases—"my streightn'd breast! my lifeless spark! my fireless flame!" also act appositively. The total result is choppy, curt.

In the stanza preceding the one quoted, the effect is much better, for Taylor does not stop his sense at the end of the line. The second line reads "O'er running it: all running o'er beside," and for the sense could end there, but it does not; it continues two monosyllables into the next line, where it ends with an exclamation. The effect is very similar to what Gerard Manley Hopkins achieves; for Taylor writes: "O'er running it: all running o'er beside / This world! Nay overflowing hell; wherein / For Thine elect, there rose a mighty tide!" The technique makes what would ordinarily be a rigid form quite flexible. By shifting the pauses or caesurae or by omitting them entirely, he can write abruptly or fairly smoothly, as he chooses. Characteristically, however, he chooses to be curt, and rarely runs more than two lines without some interruption. For intentional harshness he exaggerates the number of interruptions, mainly by running single words in series, as in Meditation 1.39, where he most successfully uses harshness to create a sense of dramatic struggle:

> My sin! My sin, my God, these cursed dregs.
>   Green, yellow, blue-streakt poison, hellish, rank,
> Bubs hatcht in nature's nest on serpent's eggs,
>   Yelp, cherp, and cry: they set my soul acramp.
> —I frown, chide, strike, and fight them, mourn and cry
>   To conquer them, but cannot them destroy.

The verse is as cramped as his soul, and it is undoubtedly meant to be so. The inversion of the last two words, also characteristic of his poetry, offers a problem: too often it is the necessary result of straining after rhymes, but many times it appears completely unprovoked. Taylor apparently felt inversion to be a legitimate mode of poetic expression.

Using the same devices as in Meditation 1.39, but beginning with two stressed monosyllables instead of the two iambs of "My sin! My sin," Taylor manages in Meditation 2.69 to slow the cadence from the opening words. Partly because of the diction, but primarily because of fewer interruptives, the roughness of this stanza is conversational rather than intensely dramatic, as in the former example:

> Dull! Dull! my Lord, as if I eaten had
>   A peck of melancholy: or my soul
> Was lockt up by a poppy key, black, sad:
>   Or had been fuddled with a henbane bowl.
> Oh, leaden temper! My rich thesis would
>   Try metal to the back, sharp, it t'unfold.

It would be interesting to know at what point the inversion "eaten had" of the first line was adopted. Perhaps it is a revision of an initial syntax to fit the word "sad" of the third line, but the third line hardly seems important enough to have merited such a change.

By removing most of the interjections, he achieves rhythmic effects that sound most modern, as in these lines from Meditation 2.80: "And if you say, What then is life? I say / I cannot tell you what it is, yet know / That various kinds of life lodge in my clay." The tone is mildly argumentative and without tangible imagery, bringing Taylor's love letters to the Lord under the same censure that befell Donne's legalistic love poems; Dryden accused Donne of perplexing "the minds of the fair sex with nice speculations of philosophy, when he should engage their hearts, and entertain them with the softness of love." But even when, as Taylor usually does, he concentrates on images, the brevity of phrase and the ruggedness of his verses keep him from attaining the mellifluence of—to choose extreme examples—a Milton or a Dylan Thomas. His poetry rarely sings.

Taylor often counteracts the asperity of his lines by manipulating images of sound within the line. Thus, though a line may be interrupted and almost broken into two half-lines, he maintains a connection between the two parts in the manner of Old English alliterative verse.

Such *r*ugged looks, // and *r*agged *r*obes I wear
(*PM*, 2.62)

. . . .

The *cl*ouds to rend, // and *sk*ies their *cr*ystal door
(*PM*, 2.92)

. . . .

My *r*avisht hea*r*t // on *r*apture's wings would fly
(*PM*, 2.93)

. . . .

*W*i*ll* ki*ll* the *w*orms // that *w*orm ho*l*e do my heart.
(*PM*, 2.84)

Put together in consecutive lines, the alliterative sounds interlock to minimize the effect of the punctuation; in the following example, the *e*, *m*, and *p* sounds link four lines:

What! shall a *m*ote u*p* to a *m*onarch rise?
An *emm*et *m*atch an *em*peror in *m*ight?
If *p*rinc*e*s make their *p*ersonal *e*xercise
Betri*mm*ing *m*ouse holes, *p*ainting with delight
(*PM*, 2.95)

Often, I think, the alliterative effect is accidental; it is the simple result of repeating key words for which, in Taylor's theological reasoning, there could be no cognates or substitutes.

But intentional repetition of words for the sake of their sound is not only characteristic of his verse but is also one of the rhetorical devices Taylor would have learned at school. Technically, he favors two figures: *ploce* and *polyptoton*. Ploce is repetition of the same word in different contexts or functioning as different parts of speech; polyptoton is the repetition of the core or base of a word modified by various affixes. Words like *love, life, Lord,* and *grace* are most successfully treated this way, as with the word *glory* in the following passage, where it occurs thirteen times in nine lines:

> The greatest *glory glory* doth enjoy,
>   Lies in her hanging upon thee, wherein
> *Glory* that *glorifies* thee mightily
>   Is far more *glorified.* Hence *glories* spring.
> Now grace's *glory,* heaven's *glory,* and
> *Glories* of saints and angels gild thy hand.
>
> A *glorious* palace, a bright crown of *glory,*
>   A *glorious* train of saints and angels' shine
> And *glorious* exercise as sweetest posy.
>
>   (*PM,* 2.73)

And the fine ecstatic passage of Meditation 1.12 slips from one meaning and form of the word *love* without appearing to "torture one poor word ten thousand ways":

> My *lovely* one, I fain would *love* thee much
>   But all my *love* is none at all I see,
> Oh! let thy beauty give a glorious touch
>   Upon my heart, and melt to *love* all me,
> Lord melt me all up into *love* for thee,
>   Whose *loveliness* excells what *love* can be.

Here the one word links three stanzas together and demonstrates the possibilities of ploce and polyptoton in connection with the favorite seventeenth-century witty exercises in paradox and oxymoron, the use of incongruous words. Thus the entire "Preface" to *God's Determinations* turns primarily on the repetition of the words *all* and *nothing.* [16]

In these "doublers," as Puttenham describes the ploce, or in his frequent "Grieve, grieve, my soul," "My sin! My sin!" or "Dull! Dull!" which Puttenham finds "not commendable,"[17] and in his exclamatory "Oh!" and parenthetical "Lord," Taylor uses repetitive means to a varied end; for all serve to vary the cadence and arrest attention at often unexpected intervals. As a result—and in combination with appositive phrases, subordinate clauses, and suspended grammatical connection—Taylor makes difficult reading. But the compactness produced by these short phrases makes Taylor's line packed or strong. Yet never, as with many exponents of the strong line, does he fall into the Senecan fallacy of seeming to say more than he actually does simply because the line is difficult to read. The obscurity of many seventeenth-century poets is often equatable with their unexpected abruptness, but I think Taylor never intended obscurity. Allowing for his grammatical license, his unusual punctuation, and his inversions, the sentence structure in Taylor's poetry is simpler than that in his sermons, primarily because he rarely runs a sentence longer than four lines.

What surprises modern readers of Taylor are not these tricks of sound, but the *inharmonious harmony* of his images. Not merely because of the actual or imagined distance between elements yoked together fiercely by metaphor, but because one of these elements is divine, modern readers react to the quaintness of Taylor's *inappropriately* homely comparisons much as did Samuel Johnson, who decried "that familiarity with religious images, and that light allusion to sacred things, by which readers far short of sanctity are frequently offended; and which would not be borne in the present age, when, devotion, perhaps not more fervent, is more delicate." Using the same figure Taylor does, Johnson describes the principles of decorum: "language is the dress of thought: and as the noblest mien or most graceful action would be degraded and obscured by a garb appropriated to the gross employments of rustics or mechanics, so the most heroic sentiments will lose their efficacy, and the most splendid ideas drop their magnificence, if they are conveyed by words used commonly upow low and trivial occasions, debased by vulgar mouths and contaminated by inelegant applications."[18] Taylor knew the principle, since his copy of John Weemes's *The Christian Synagogue* clearly advises against drawing comparisons from "things altogether different" or "unfit," and also points out specifically:

If thou wouldst praise a thing, take the Comparison from stately things, as in the Canticles.
If thou wouldst dispraise, take your comparison from base things.[19]

But another theory seems to have predominated in the English meditative tradition. George Herbert calls attention to the Bible's sanction of "base things," since the Holy Ghost there "condescends to the naming of a plough, a hatchet, a bushell, leaven, boyes piping and dancing; shewing that things of ordinary use are not only to serve in the way of drudgery, but to be washed, and cleansed, and serve for lights even of Heavenly Truths."[20] Bishop Hall turns the fact to precept by commenting that what "we are wont to say of fine wits, we may as truly affirm of the Christian heart, that it can make use of any thing."[21] And Richard Baxter urges even more strongly that "we might have a fuller tast of Christ and Heaven, in every bit of bread that we eat, and in every draught of Beer that we drink, then most men have in the use of the sacrament."[22] Surprisingly, Baxter anticipates Taylor's excited identification of the sacramental wine: "It's beer! No nectar like it," a beer "Wrought in the Spirit's brew house." And so, regarding the most elevated of subjects, Taylor's poems abound in cockle-shells, tobacco and tinder boxes, leather coats, trenchers, bowling balls, tents, needles, yarn and spinning wheels, canoes, bullets, and lobster claws.

Strangely, Taylor's use of the entire realm of nature never results in any fresh look at nature itself; and he is, therefore, less a poet of nature than Bradstreet. Furthermore, there is a tendency among mystical writers to make nature sacramental; to find a sacredness in natural objects because of God's imprint there; and to fall, in fact, into pantheism; the absence of this characteristic in Taylor is rather surprising. "Every little ice-cycle is the workmanship of God," says Cotton Mather, wonderingly; Jonathan Edwards describes the new joy in nature after his conversion as ecstatically, if not as well, as Wordsworth; and John Woolman's descriptions reveal a sympathy for natural things unmatched to that time in American writing. But in spite of Taylor's stated preference for natural over artificial things, the nature of his *Meditations* exists as if it were in an allegorical tapestry. Its objects are purely symbolic, isolated from all natural environment, and interesting primarily as an illustration of some moral.[23]

Only once, in fact, does Taylor describe a natural phenomenon as if he wished to capture its nature rather than to apply it to some other use:

> This pale-fac'd moon that silver snowball like,
>   That walks in'ts silver glory, paints the skies,
> The tester of the bed, where day and night,
>   Each creature cover'd o'er with glory lies,

> She with her silver rays envarnish doth
> In silver paint, the skies as out she go'th.
>
> (*PM*, 2.99)

The description's porcelain brittleness might have appeared in an Elizabethan sonnet; but, where Sidney's moon mounts with sad steps, Taylor's merely walks, paints, and varnishes the skies with silver. The actions become human actions without the moon's being personified. And in the next stanza the moon's prettiness fades in the glory of the Sun of Righteousness, whose beams are "her tapestry / Which gilds the heavens o'er, hung out on high."

Taylor's descriptions of the sky contain this same quality: it is a bowling alley, golden battlements, the "paintice" of a tent, "Heav'ns whelm'd-down crystal meal bowl," heaven's curtains, a lantern holding a candle, a crystal roof, the earth's canopy, or some other very tangible stage backdrop for divine actions. Always the metaphor is either scriptural or in terms of household objects: curtains, lanterns, roofs, bowls. The effect of this is, on the one hand, to elevate and dignify "base" objects; on the other, to steal magnificence and sublimity from the subject.

Although Taylor ranges widely for details, five general classes of images recur with notable frequency. The first class—writing images, including remarks on rhetoric, metaphor, and duty—I have already discussed.[24] Although such images commonly open *Meditations*—just as the gamut of musical instruments closes them—they often function as central images around which Taylor structures the argument of a whole poem. The second group of images is of warfare; and most often Taylor employs the assault of the fort of life—as in a Spenserian allegory—replete with soldiers, scouts, generals, bombardments, mortars, bullets. The attack may be engineered by Satan or by Christ, Taylor may picture himself enlisted under Christ's standard, or the shepherd's crook may become a mace. These images of combat are closely related to the third class: those of metallurgy, mining, trying ore or distilling, and minting. These all suggest purification, testing, or trying for purity; the removal of impurities; or the alchemical transformation from one state to another. Alembics and try-pots, anvils, the face of Christ printed on the pure gold of the poet's coin, the conversion of lead to gold—all these belong under this category; and they identify Taylor with the Hermetic—or magical—sources of mystical imagery.[25] The monetary image leads naturally to images of treasures and purses,

betting, and commerce; and the commercial imagery prepares the
ground for the legal action and the advocates and the judges which are
common in seventeenth-century lyrics. The categories tend, therefore,
to extend themselves beyond neat limits.

But two classes of images predominate—gardens and feasts. Gardens
flourish throughout mystical literature,[26] for they are an imaginative
extension of the Garden of Eden. Taylor's garden images vary widely—
formal knots, individual flowers, herbs, seeds, slips and cuttings,
grafts, vines and trees, blossoms and fruits. And any of these may
suggest new lines of imagery. Herbs, for example, being medicinal,
often lead Taylor quickly from the garden to the apothecary's shop. His
gardens almost always suggest the one of John's Revelations, but it is
curiously removed to New England, where grains as well as flowers
abound. The saints are the choice grain compared to which Taylor often
feels himself to be the bran, chaff, husk, or shell. Related to the grain
image is a series of images about the processes of grinding, kneading,
and baking that turn the grain into the bread of life to be served at the
Lord's Supper; or those about the pressing, distilling, and brewing
procedures that convert the garden's grapes to sacramental brew. In this
way the garden imagery moves naturally to the second major class, the
images of the feast.

The surprising extent and the nature of Taylor's feast imagery are
among the most striking features of the *Meditations*. The wedding feast
celebrating the union of man and God was, as I have noted abundantly,
the nexus of Taylor's faith. Since it was also the occasion and the reason
for the *Meditations* themselves, it seems not unusual that images of
eating and drinking should occur plenteously. But again Taylor's trick
of converting the spiritual proceedings to domestic naturalism has a
startling effect:

> Here is a feast indeed! in ev'ry dish
>   A whole redeemer, cooked up bravely, good,
> Is served up in holy sauce that is
>   A mess of delicates made of his blood.
>   Adorn'd with grace's sippits: rich sweet-meats.
>   Comfort and comforts sweeten whom them eats.
>
>   (*PM*, 2.108)

Grace personified does the honors: carves, rolls the meat in the sauce,
and fattens the souls of the partakers. Taylor takes extreme advantage of

cannibalistic ritual: "What!" he exclaims, "feed on human flesh and blood? Strange mess!" Nature calls this custom barbarous, and scripture finds it inadmissible; therefore, it must be interpreted symbolically, metaphorically. But once the symbol is introduced, he takes complete license with the metaphor: Christ's body is heaven's sugar cake, sweet junkets, Zion's pastry, griddle-cakes baked in God's bakehouse, roast meat, or plum cake. Christ's blood is wine, beer, nectar, or the drippings from the roast, into which the saints dip holy biscuits.

As shocking and tasteless as this image appears to modern readers, it is really almost commonplace in Renaissance and earlier devotional writing. In it—and for that matter in Saint Augustine—appear the grinding of divine flour, the baking of bread for Communion, and the wine-press as a symbol of the breaking and converting of Christ's body. The following passage from Taylor is, therefore, really less quaint in writing of its kind than it appears to us. He is considering Christ as the True Vine:

> Her grapes when pounded and presst hard (hard fare)
> Bleed out both blood and spirit, leaving none,
> Which too much took, the brain doth too much toll,
> Tho't smacks the palate, merry makes the soul.
>
> (*PM,* 2.98)

In this quotation it is not the wine-press figure that is unusual with Taylor; it is the gustatory smacking and the titillation of the soul.

Like the images of the banquet, bread, and the wine press, all of Taylor's symbols are conventional in devotional literature. Only his strange eye for peculiar details, his going one step beyond the convention, and his domesticating his symbols with kitchen details give his symbolism a quaint, sometimes grotesque, individual quality. But even Taylor's manner of treating his imagery indicates the specific source from which it was drawn. For, from the time of the publication of Geoffrey Whitney's *A Choice of Emblemes* (1586), the emblem as a formal, semi-literary device became influential in English literature. Emblem books proper consisted of collections of engravings or woodcuts of moral symbols; attached to each picture was a motto or sententia explicating the drawn symbol. Each picture was also accompanied by a short poem or prose passage interpreting and moralizing from the picture and its motto.[27] The symbols pictured were largely medieval—a skeleton or skull or headstone representing death, an anchor for hope, a wheel for occasion or fortune—and they appeared either singly or related to other symbols. The more complex the relationship of symbols, the more necessary became the accompanying prose or poetry. Likewise, the poem so required the picture that it was often unintelligible without it.

By the time of Taylor's youth the emblem books had been fully exploited in the interests of religious devotion. Francis Quarles and George Wither, both highly respected among New Englanders and generally among middle-class Puritan groups, published books of this kind. Quarles's *Emblemes* (1635) and *Hieroglyphikes of the Life of Man* (1638), which were extremely popular, offer some close resemblances to Taylor's later practice. For, while Quarles changes his form and even his manner from narrative to dialogue to personal lyric, the basis of most of his poems is—like Taylor's—the soul aspiring to heaven; or, more particularly, the soul is personified as Anima seeking and being sought by Divine Love.

The pictures accompanying Quarles's poems make it most obvious that an earlier emblem subject, the adventures of Cupid, has been transmogrified to religious ends. Rosemary Freeman describes the change most clearly: "By a simple transference the whole idiom was absorbed into a devotional framework: Cupid became the infant Jesus or Divine Love seeking the human soul, personified in Anima, a young maiden."[28] These are the major figures of Quarles's pictures, and around them are associated the symbolic devices—anchors, skeletons, lilies, roses, arrows piercing hearts, and so on. Consequently, Quarles often assumes—as in the following—the female rôle in the poems, very much as Taylor does:

> Nor Time, nor Place, nor Chance, nor Death can bow
>   My least desires unto the least remove;
> He's firmly mine by oath; I his by vow;
>   He's mine by faith; and I am his by love;
>   He's mine by water; I am his by wine;
> Thus I my best-beloved's am; thus he is mine.[29]

But what Quarles gains in smoothness he lacks in fervor and intensity; he never attains the ardent personal feelings Taylor infuses into his best *Meditations*.

In another way, however, the emblems of Quarles are most important. They are based on two of the many such books sponsored by

Jesuits,[30] who were not only ultimately responsible for Taylor's meditative method but for distributing emblem books designed primarily to assist exercitants in that method.[31] In these books appear the hearts, gardens, alembics, lilies, roses, candles, lanterns, sweeping of rooms, weapons, trees, and Old Testament "types" that Taylor employs and that served as a body of conventional images from which the emblem writer worked. Protestants, turning these Catholic devices to their own use, retained the pictures from Catholic books that were not too inimical to their own theology and then wrote new accompanying poems.

In this way the habit of emblematic thought became significantly widespread among English religious poets. Donne's famed compass image derives from the emblem books. George Herbert's manner of treating physical objects such as the church floor, the windows, the pulleys—which was so congenial to Crashaw, Vaughan, and Traherne—is also the fashion of the emblematists; and it is, therefore, less surprising that Taylor often reminds readers of these poets. But emblems were not only a part of the study of rhetoric; they were also a prominent feature of the decorative arts generally in the England of Taylor's youth. Jewelry, domestic decorations, architectural ornaments, and, most significantly for Taylor, needlework and tapestry— all habitually used emblems as subjects or motifs.[32] Taylor could not have escaped these symbols.

In two ways the emblem manner influenced Taylor's poetry: one is the analytical approach to the allegorical symbols; the other, visualization. Quarles, for example, presents an engraving depicting a shipwreck. Only the stern and one mast of a vessel remain above water, poised for their final plunge; and, in the background, a vicious dart of lightning snakes its way into a stormy sea. In the foreground a smiling survivor swims toward a rocky haven where a winged and radiant figure leans forward to save the swimmer. In spite of the storm and darkness, the smile on the face of the survivor and the imminence of salvation turn the mood from violent desperation to calm assurance.[33] The accompanying poem, based on a text from Pss. 69:15, "Let not the waterflood overflow me, neither let the deeps swallow me up," actually supplies many physical details not evident in the engraving itself and it traces a point-by-point meaning of the symbolism:

> The world's a Sea; my flesh a ship that's mann'd
> With lab'ring Thoughts, and steer'd by Reason's hand:
> My Heart's the Sea-man's Card, whereby she sails;

> My loose Affections are the greater Sails:
> The Top-sail is my Fancie, and the Gusts
> That fill these wanton sheets are worldly Lusts.
> Pray'r is the Cable, at whose end appears
> The Anchor Hope, nev'r slipt but in our fears:
> My Will's th'unconstant Pilot, that commands
> The stagg'ring Keel; my sinnes are like the Sands:
> Repentance is the Bucket, and mine Eye
> The Pump, unus'd (but in extremes) and dry.[34]

Quarles continues to identify the details for several lines; then, repeating the catalog, he indicates that each of the details—cable, anchor,
pilot—is somehow faulty; and finally, going through the list a third
time, he petitions the Lord to correct each where it fails:

> Make strong my Cable; bind my Anchor faster;
> Direct my Pilot, and be thou his Master;
> Object the Sands to my more serious view,
> Make sound my Bucket, bore my Pump anew:

Especially in this last section of the poem, but even in its earlier two,
we find the technique of extending a conceit by an analytic comparison
of its parts; and this is precisely what we also find in a number of
Taylor's *Preparatory Meditations*[35] and in "Huswifery" in particular:

> Make me, O Lord, thy spinning wheel complete.
> Thy Holy Word my distaff make for me.
> Make mine affections thy swift flyers neat
> And make my soul thy holy spool to be.
> My conversation make to be thy reel
> And reel the yarn thereon spun of thy wheel.

But the point-by-point anatomy of a central image is not so common
in Taylor's poetry as "Huswifery" suggests. Taylor's concern is with
anatomizing ideas rather than images; and the abrupt shift from one
image to another quite disparate one is more characteristic of his verse.
But the emblematic quality of visualization marks the poems even
when this other method is dropped. He seems to imagine not only
particulars clearly but also the peculiar allegorical relation they fell into
so naturally in emblem drawings. This characteristic obviates the diffi-

culty Professor Warren finds in such lines as the following where the Rose apparently "at once invites and repels visualization."[36]

> Shall heaven and earth's bright glory all up lie
> Like sunbeams bundled in the sun in thee?
> Dost thou sit Rose at table head, where I
> Do sit, and carv'st no morsel sweet for me?

The idea of the Rose of Sharon carving at table repels visualization only if conceived naturalistically; it is unnatural and illogical at first appearance. Seen, however, as an emblematist would see it, the rose at the head of a feast-laden table, surrounded by carving utensils, and radiating lines like sunbeans from the sun, is most plausible symbolically. And it is in this way that Taylor's *Meditations* are emblematic: they depend upon an imaginary drawing which is perfectly clear in Taylor's imagination; but, because understanding his images involves a mode of thought unfamiliar to modern readers, they are difficult for us to picture.[37] His most conventional emblems—the paintings of death which he describes in Meditations 1.34 and 2.112 as complete with skeleton, hourglass, and spade—offer no such difficulty because of their perpetual appropriateness.

Taylor transcends the emblem tradition at the same time that he uses it to full advantage in *Meditations;* and he achieves this transcendence not only by his individual visualization of highly traditional allegorical symbols, but also by his joining the visual with other senses. I know of no other poet who so fully resorts to other than visual imagery, for Taylor runs the full range. His feast not only looks like bread and wine or roast and sauce, but smells and tastes like it. Tactile sensations of snarled and ragged cloth and of a host of irritants—chaffing, grinding, pricking—contribute to his poetic texture. Incense, flowers, and pillars of perfumes reek heavily through the *Meditations*—and far more prominently than in other poets. Crashaw's fluid images of milk, blood, and tears are almost matched by Taylor. Birds, saints, angels, and a symphony of musical instruments swell his verse with twangs and tweedles, hymns, carols, and songs of praise, as his tabor stick drums at the company of ears. And kinesthetic sensations of wallowing, submersion, elevation, careening through the air, soaring, and even bouncing like a tennis ball round out Taylor's sensory world. The fullness of this feature of Taylor's verse is, however, less obvious in single poems; but a sustained reading of the *Meditations* makes it readily apparent.

The world of the *Meditations* storms constantly with an impressive variety of shapes, colors, odors, and feelings. The effect is rich and ornate; but, like stained glass or medieval illuminations, it is strangely two-dimensional. Foreground and background are treated with equal attention, given equal scope. The perspective is unnatural, for earth and heaven impinge one upon another with a boldness at once medieval and cubistic or surrealistic. The *Meditations* become a tapestry-like setting, antique and modern at the same time, which makes a most suitable backdrop for the miracle play enacted before it.

God's Determinations

In Taylor's one extended attempt to imbue this poetic world with life, he created a perplexing drama of grace, drawing into concert a full range of emotional, sensational, and intellectual experiences he explored individually in the *Meditations*. *God's Determinations Touching His Elect: and the Elect's Combat in their Conversion and Coming up to God in Christ, together with the Comfortable Effects thereof* has been dismissed as "a labor of versified doctrine," but it has also been applauded for its lyric performance that is "far beyond anything achieved by Americans until long after Taylor's day.[38] Because the overall poem is so fragmented, because it presents such a medley of varying voices, and because its central figure of the Elect Soul is psychologically split into a variety of allegorical projections, a reader is likely to feel displaced into the world of William Carlos Williams's *Paterson* rather than into seventeenth-century New England.

Works of this kind, both in prose and verse, common enough in Taylor's time, were known as rhapsodies—a purposely ragged stitching together of sometimes quite disparate materials. Such purposeful disunity—what Melville called in his great rhapsody "a careful disorderliness"—can have disconcerting effects, hinting first at one kind of literary expectation and then quickly at another. It is possible to see *God's Determinations* more usefully in terms of musical models than literary ones—each voice differentiated and identified by its own register and style, its own stanzaic identity, all of them orchestrated toward a conclusion in sound that reinforces the logical order of the title. If the *Meditations* often seem like blind emblems—the pictorial element missing—*God's Determinations* is most like a cantata or a chamber opera whose music has been incorporated into the sound-

patterns of the verse. Claudio Monteverdi, who died the year after
Taylor was born, and Antonio Vivaldi, whose life overlapped Taylor's
(1678–1741), offer excellent examples of these forms, a small assem-
blage of voices distributed into recitative, arias, solos, duets, and
ensembles—often, as in Vivaldi's *Dixit,* on scriptural texts.

But the poem also echoes other more familiar poetic kinds—the song
cycles of loosely but purposely arranged lyrics, such as Herbert's *The
Temple;* the morality play of the kind Taylor may have seen as a youth in
Leicestershire; the verse-sermon; or a fully developed meditation in the
Ignatian mode, an expanded version of his own *Preparatory Meditations.*
Elements of each prevail by turns, but one is likely to be immediately
impressed by the virtuosity with which Taylor employs and plays with
the full range of his accomplishments as a poet. Certainly the thirty-
five poems of *God's Determinations* illustrate all that Taylor achieved in
his other verse. The iambic pentameter couplets of the elegies appear in
them with considerably more vividness and excitement than elsewhere,
varied occasionally by division into *aabb* quatrains as a vehicle for
dialogue. The couplets are offset by six-line stanzaic verse rhymed
ababcc, as in the *Meditations,* but these stanzas are sometimes altered
metrically. In all, Taylor uses eleven different verse forms and plays
with such unifying devices as refrain, incremental repetition, and
rhyme to pull poems, or parts of poems, closely together.

"A Dialogue between Justice and Mercy," which is near the beginning of the work, is an exchange of stanzas between the two speakers
which illustrates Taylor's use of repetition and interlocking to give
continuity to the poem. Stanza 4, spoken by Justice, begins: "My
essence is ingag'd, I cannot 'bate, / Justice not done no justice is."
Mercy matches Justice in the next stanza: "My essence is engag'd pity
to show. / Mercy not done no mercy is"; but Mercy counters Justice
from there on. Stanza 9 ends with Justice's challenge to Mercy: "Then
stand away, and let me strike at first: / For better now, than when he's
at the worst." Mercy, who ends the next stanza with the same words,
turns them against Justice: "Then stand away, and strike not at the
first. / He'll better grow when he is at the worst." The next two stanzas
are linked the same way, but with different couplets:

JUSTICE

Nay, this ten thousand times as much can still
Confer no honey to the sinner's hive.

> For man, though shrived thoroughly from all ill,
>   His righteousness is merely negative.
> Though none be damned but such as sin imbrace:
> Yet none are saved without Inherent Grace.

MERCY

> What though ten thousand times too little be?
>   I will ten thousand times more do.
> I will not only from his sin him free,
>   But fill him with Inherent Grace also.
> Though none are saved that wickedness imbrace,
> Yet none are damned that have Inherent Grace.

Stanzas 13 and 14 are similarly linked, but by the first two verses only. The interlocking is made rigid here by also picking up the fifth verse of stanza 13—"Then though he's spared at first, at last he'll fall"—and echoing it as the last line of stanza 14—"Spare him at first, then he'll not fall at last." But these devices are never related one to another; they unify only parts of the dialogue, but not all, or even a major part of it. In this way the dialogue demonstrates, moreover, the erratic structure and inconsistencies of the entire work.

An incremental refrain begins the first of the concluding six lyrics, but it peters out in the last three stanzas. Like Meditation 2.95, the poem titled "The Glory of and Grace in the Church Set Out" ends the first four stanzas with the Donne-like refrain, "Yet that's not all," and it clinches the series in the final stanza with "And that's but all." In this poem Taylor sustains the refrain much more neatly throughout; and he also most successfully uses a two-verse incremental refrain to weave the final poem of *God's Determinations* together. But these stylistic reminders of the *Meditations* are insignificant in *God's Determinations* as a whole; for in the latter the individuality of the separate poems remains a far more distinct feature of a work which is primarily lyric in structure rather than narrative or dramatic. It is almost as if Taylor anticipated the romantic theories of Coleridge and Poe that there can be no such thing as a long poem—or that even the *Iliad* is "a series of lyrics."

One excuse for these breaks in the continuity of the whole is that the verse variations represent a change either in mode or in speaker. Couplets are his normal vehicle for exposition or narrative, and he interlards his dialogues with them quite unconventionally. Satan speaks couplets, as do the harassed souls who address him; and so does the Saint; but as his arguments grow more convincing, he speaks in the meditation-stanza form. Christ, who speaks only twice, uses two varieties of a stanza rhymed *aabccb*. And finally, as the three ranks of elect souls accept their fellowship in Christ, they utter six songs; each one is structurally different, and the last—"The Joy of Church Fellowship Rightly Attended"— returns to the same familiar meditative form that begins the entire work, "The Prologue" (if we follow Johnson's positioning of the poems rather than Stanford's).[39] The neatness of this principle of closure, which Wright suggests Taylor grasped from the morality plays without actually adopting their practice, is offset by the formality of the speeches; it minimizes the chance for dramatic exchange. The greatest energy comes, in fact, from the narrative passages.

Insofar as development through speeches calls for dramatic analysis, Wright finds a four-part plot: a prologue; man's fall (poems 2–6); the dialogue on salvation (poems 7–29); and a choral epilogue (the last six poems).[40] We might also see the work as a five-act drama. Act 1 sets man's predicament; it traces the Creation and the Fall and then digresses to enact the covenant of redemption in the "Dialogue between Justice and Mercy." The scene is a flashback to God's eternal will, which existed prior to the act of Creation in *God's Determinations.* In the two scenes that follow, man—unable to answer for his faults—is banished from God's favor; divided into two parts, one is invited to climb into a royal coach (at once Christ and his mystical body the church) to be carried to a glorious banquet (the Lord's Supper); the other, the rejected, sculls to eternal woe in one line. The act ends as Justice, Mercy, and Grace put into action their plan to redeem man.

Man is at the beginning one person, obviously Adam; he remains so until Taylor's description of "The Frowardness of the Elect in the Work of Conversion," where he fractures into four aspects of the conversion experience according to degrees of difficulty: (1) the Saints who surrender at once to Grace and enter the coach; (2) the elect souls—the first rank—who resist initially but yield when pressed by God's Mercy; (3) elect souls—the second rank—who are persuaded only by the assaults of God's Justice; and (4) the elect souls—the third rank—who capitulate only to the combined forces of Mercy and Justice. Because each of these four is an aspect of "man," the problem is to render identity and relationship at the same time. All four give in, as they must, for God's grace is irresistible. The first act ends with the conclusion of this conflict.

Act 2 introduces a new antagonist and a new conflict, for Satan roars out to undo the work of conversion. In the first scene—from "Satan's Rage at them in their Conversion" to "The Effect of this Reply"—four poems trace Satan's violent accusation that all three reluctant ranks are traitors, cowards, and feeblehearted; then those ranks, joined together in the speaker "Soul," question Christ; Christ's stirring assurance follows; and the effect of Christ's reply is delineated—it cheers the souls saved by Mercy (the first rank) but leaves the other two drooping. Satan turns his attack rather subtly not against these weaker ranks but against the first; in scene 2 he accuses the inward temptations, the outward sinfulness, and even the selfish motives behind the first rank's worship of God. The badgered Soul (now limited to the first rank) withstands Satan firmly, but he petitions Christ in scene 3—"The Soul's Groan to Christ for Succour"—to rid him of the tempter. Christ replies soothingly, and the scene ends with the Soul's ecstatic expression of joy— with what is really a series of contrasts between what the soul can do and what to Christ is due:

> Had I ten thousand times ten thousand hearts:
> And every heart ten thousand tongues
> To praise, I should but stutt odd parts
> Of what to thee belongs.

The second conflict concluded, the second act also ends.

In Act 3 Satan abruptly accuses the second and third ranks, since his plan to weaken them further by troubling the first rank has been spoiled. He argues entirely from the point of their failings and the justice of their destruction. After a lengthy threnody, they throw themselves into the sea of God's mercy. This tactic sustains them temporarily, and they decide at the end of Act 3 to search Mercy's golden stacks of remedies, "and of the pious wise some council take."

In Act 4 the saints who entered the coach immediately upon Grace's urging return to the center of the action. The act begins as the Soul (still representing the combined second and third ranks) confesses its spiritual disturbance because of the doubts Satan has stirred about its worthiness to receive God's favor from the hand either of Justice or Mercy. The Saint confutes all of Satan's arguments and unmasks his devious and sophistical tricks; he then calls attention to the difficulties that arise from the ill behavior of Christians. As the Saint rises into the verse form of the *Meditatations,* the second and third ranks are moved to rapturous resolutions: "Oh! let us then sing praise! methinks I soar /

Above the stars, and stand at heaven's door." But this is not the end of the act, for in the next poem the two ranks join in a duet singing "Our Insufficiency to Praise God Suitably for His Mercy." Theme and melody remind us that this is precisely the effect conversion had upon the first rank of reluctant saints at the end of Act 2, for the response of Act 4 exactly parallels the earlier one:

> Nay, had each song as many tunes most sweet,
>   Or one intwisting in't as many,
>   As all these tongues have songs most meet
>   Unparalleled by any?
> Each tongue would tune a world of praise, we guess,
> Whose songs in number would be numberless.
>
> Now should all these conspire in us that we
>   Could breathe such praise to thee, most high?
>   Should we thy sounding organs be
>   To ring such melody?
> Our music would the world of worlds outring,
> Yet be unfit within thine ears to sing.

This duet functions as both the conclusion to Act IV and the opening movement of the choral epilogue—as Wright terms it—that is Act V. In the poem that follows—"The Soul Seeking Church-Fellowship"— Taylor shifts back to the narrative recitative of the first act. The Soul, who is the subject of this dramatic song, is once again the collective voice of all four of its aspects, the quartet that now shyly accepts its collective selection among the favored of God. As in the *Meditations,* the object of desire—fellowship with saints and angels in the church— shifts unexpectedly from a garden to a city before the original image of the royal coach reappears; the Soul first timorously and then joyously enters it, and sings Christ's praises as it soars up to its banquet of love in heaven.

If we view these last six poems as a single unit, we discover that they describe the general threefold pattern of the individual *Preparatory Meditations:* (1) statement or question, (2) development, and (3) final petition or praise. It is as if each of these poems were a single stanza in a long *Meditation.* As in so many of the *Meditations,* this one begins by asserting the soul's "Insufficiency to Praise God Suitably for His Mercy." The souls are described as mould and nettles, anticipating the garden imagery of the first poem of the development section, "The Soul

Seeking Church-Fellowship." Also, as in the development section of
the *Meditations,* the central image shifts; from the garden of "The Soul
Seeking Church-Fellowship" it becomes the glorious city of "The Soul
Admiring the Grace of the Church"; and it then goes back to the
garden knot of "The Glory of and Grace in the Church Set Out."
Though the image shifts, the argument is single: the Soul, torn between its fear of unworthiness and its desire for marriage with Christ,
uncertainly enters the "coach of God's decree" and so supplants fear
with joy. This conflict between uncertainty and longing is the emotional basis of most of the *Meditations.*

Even after the Soul of *God's Determinations* enters the church, her
misgivings about her own weaknesses ("The Soul's Admiration Hereupon") continue to plague her. As Taylor does in the *Meditations,* the
Soul here continues her self-deprecation in terms of an unskilled musi-
cian or an untuned musical instrument. "The Soul's Admiration Hereupon" and the final "Joy of Church Fellowship Rightly Attended"
function like the last stanza of a *Meditation,* but in these poems the
hypothetical element is removed. In the *Meditations,* the Soul promises
to sing God's praises *if* he helps her; the final poem of *God's Determinations* describes both God's help and God's praises as accomplished facts.
The souls are 'encoacht for heaven," wheeling there melodiously; and,
in their mystical union with the body of Christ, they have fully attained
the unitive life:

> In all their acts, public and private, nay,
> And secret, too, they praise impart,
> But in their acts divine and worship, they
> With hymns do offer up their heart.
>
> (11. 19–22)

These last six poems, then, make up a statement of moved affections,
a response to the convincing truth of the arguments presented by the
Saint in Act IV and implicit in the total action of *God's Determinations,*
which is a drama of conflict within the soul. As a unit these last six
poems relate to the rest of the work just as Taylor's individual *Meditations* do to their preceding sermons. *God's Determinations* is thus itself a
formal Ignatian meditation: the opening act corresponds to Loyola's
historical prelude and composition of place, vividly imagined, particularly described; the debates with Satan and the advice of the Saint are

Loyola's "points of consideration" and Baxter's "Discourse of Minde";
and the final poems are the colloquy or response of moved affections.
The advantage of this view of *God's Determinations* is that it minimizes the dramatic demands of the work as a whole; justifies to some
extent the theological argumentation; and relates the work, in spirit as
in form, with the primary enterprise of Taylor's devotional life. It need
not take full advantage of its dramatic elements but it can use them to
lend vivacity to the meditation, which is why several Renaissance
devotional books resort to dialogue. Meditation also permits the ar-
rangement of theological considerations very similar to that of Taylor's
sermons. When the Saint turns to advise troubled souls in Act 4, he
really comes to apply the doctrine of grace as in the application of the
sermon, commending them to watch themselves, fear not, and be
forward in the service of God.

But most important, *God's Determinations*—whether perceived as a
song cycle, chamber opera, morality play, or meditation—is finally an
extended, ambitious literary work, bringing together in one artistic
effort all of Taylor's techniques and concerns. It is neither a spontane-
ous effusion nor an occasion-bound duty, as were the *Meditations*. Yet
its ideas, versification, and movement, its identical images and wording, its similar methods of development, and its parallel structures all
testify to the abiding spirit of the *Meditations*. In *God's Determinations*
we also find Taylor's progress of the soul from its crippled, lapsed estate
to the heavenly banquet; the necessity of allegorical reading; the self-
deprecation and continual fear of hypocrisy; the anatomy of the soul in
self-examination; the insistence upon purity before admission to the
church; the mystical marriage; and even the anti-Stoddardean arguments about the assurance with which the Lord's Supper should be
approached. Since the feast itself is never described but always anticipated, we can call *God's Determinations*, like the *Meditations*, "preparatory." In the 2,107 verses of *God's Determinations* the private and public
voices entwine into something more than song—into what Walt Whit-
man later called the "budding bibles" of New Worlds.

Chapter Five
Appraisal

The dust jacket to the 1939 Rockland edition of Taylor's *Poetical Works* trumpeted "that a reevaluation of early American letters will be made in the light of this publication." Nearly fifty years later, that claim seems too modest; since Taylor emerged in print, our entire notion of American Puritan culture has been radically revised. Coincidentally, 1939 also saw the first publication of Perry Miller's absolutely dominating *The New-England Mind: The Seventeenth Century,* which provided intellectual underpinnings for the commonplace observation that New England's culture was cheerless, grim, and colorless. That had been Hawthorne's view and Longfellow's, and who better for later historians—Moses Coit Tyler, Vernon L. Parrington, Louis B. Wright, Samuel Eliot Morison, Kenneth B. Murdock—to follow?

Intelligent, informed, urbane, and stylistically brilliant, these historians attended to colonial literature only with varying degrees of condescension. Miller did not condescend, however, and instead showed that Puritan literature, understood as a body of ideas with a history, was not only crucially important for reaching an understanding of the American mind, but also capable of generating the highest kind of intellectual excitement. He anatomized the seventeenth-century mind's piety, psychology, theology, and sociology so masterfully that for a generation it seemed impossible to think outside of Miller's dicta. Everything was suddenly clearer, and literature assumed an unexpected importance in the process. But poetry did not. Miller seemed to show that because his Puritan mind valued intellect over emotion, logic above desire, and use before pleasure, a genuine Puritan poetry would be an oxymoron.

But Taylor's poetry presented a problem. If Miller's description of Puritan aesthetics were correct, then there could be no Edward Taylor. Either that, or Taylor was no Puritan. Miller never did get a genuine grasp of Taylor, opting as many other prominent historians did for the depiction of Taylor as a closet Catholic, furtively composing his ardent poems in secret, practicing both poetic heresy and Protestant heresy at once. The 1954 edition of *The New-England Mind* reinforced that view of Taylor the hypocrite of the forest, as did anthologies in that decade, including Miller's own *The American Puritans*. With the fuller view of Taylor's *Poems* presented in Stanford's edition of 1960, and with the publication of the *Christographia*, it became abundantly clear, however, that the public Taylor differed little, if at all, in ideas and styles from the private Taylor, that his orthodoxy was beyond question, and that his sinister secrecy existed only in the minds of historians.

Not only did Miller's aesthetic almost entirely collapse in the presence of Taylor, it became quickly clear that the aesthetic was inadequate for evaluating some other examples of Puritan art, too. Allan I. Ludwig established that truth by examining the audacious, erotic, flamboyant, and witty imagery of New England gravestone carvings. Had these been thought heretical, they would never have been commissioned in the first place; had they violated Puritan standards of faith, taste, and decorum, the offensive images would have been vandalized and mutilated by contemporaries. But up they went, standing whole for the main part, subject primarily to the criticism of time and weather. Taylor's aesthetic was literally carved in stone.[1]

Ludwig's book illustrates the great shift in historical attention that has occurred since the sixties. Increasingly the object of historians' attention has become group or class behavior—the family, the town, the demos. Not every Puritan went to Harvard. Not every Puritan wrote books, let alone poems. Obviously a cultural history based only upon the evidence provided by literate, educated, intellectual, and professional makers of books will be a warped, an elite cultural history. It might be accurate, in a way, but it could only express one strand of New England culture. What might other, less verbal kinds of evidence—voting patterns, town development, trading practices, distribution of wealth, marriage constraints—have to tell us? How might Ludwig's graven images announce the ideas of the ordinary citizen in Taylor's time? Ideas do not have men, insisted Larzer Ziff in 1973; it is men who have ideas.[2] The concept of a totally collective "mind," superior to all the quirky individuals and human groups composing it, simply ceased to command attention and interest. Partly, of course, this situation merely describes a shift in intellectual fashion among historians, who found demographics newly intriguing; partly it reflects the need to find new kinds of evidence and new arrangements of it suited to the theoretical models of Claude Lévi-Strauss, Michel Foucault, and Clifford Geertz; and partly it represents the continuing and strengthening pull of Marxist social analysis as practiced by scholars such as Raymond Williams. How exciting and valuable this recent movement is can be seen in the collection of fifteen retrospective essays by leading colonial historians brought together by Jack P. Greene and J. R. Pole in 1984—*Colonial British America: Essays in the New History of the Early Modern Era.* The collection contains no essay on colonial literature, and Edward Taylor does not even appear in the index.[3]

"No ideas but in things," claimed William Carlos Williams, the champion of modern objectivism. Our recent historians agree, but while Williams saw poems as things, historians do not, rather easily disregarding literature as an element of historical culture. Literary historians have, in their way, also responded to recent objectivist interests, but have done so without relinquishing a concern for aesthetic values and interpretation. Perhaps that is why so much of the labor devoted to Taylor since 1960 has come in the form of editing Taylor's poetry and prose, a task made daunting by the decrepit condition of the manuscripts. By 1970, still propelled by Thomas H. Johnson's tasteful and judicious selections, scholars had made available all the major poetry and much of the minor, the *Christographia* sermons, the *Treatise Concerning the Lord's Supper,* and a few letters. In the seventies bibliographies (by Grabo, Constance Gevfert, and Scheick and Doggett) began to display and vivify the deepening appreciation of Taylor. In 1981 Thomas M. and Virginia L. Davis brought together Taylor's previously unpublished work in three substantial volumes called *Unpublished Writings of Edward Taylor.* These include sermons and records relating to the Westfield church and to Taylor's protracted engagement with the Stoddardean controversy, and all the minor poems. Clearly labors of love as well as learning, these volumes will affect our sense of Taylor beyond prediction, and, of course, so will Charles W. Mignon's long-awaited edition of Taylor's thirty-six sermons jointly called *Upon the Types of the Old Testament,* a thousand-page manuscript discovered in a secondhand bookstore in Lincoln, Nebraska, in 1977.[4]

As this work accumulates and unfolds for public study, it enables us to see more sharply and more delicately into the complex possibilities inherent in Puritan aesthetics. At first view Taylor simply dazzled his readers. Nothing like him had been seen in America. Not strangely, then, some early readers—conscious of his nonspecific locale and diction, and not fully alert to the special Americanness of early Congregationalism—protested that he had no place in the canon of American poetry. If he belonged anywhere, they argued, it was among the English metaphysical poets he so closely resembled. But the new breed of college anthologists who published after World War II were quick to follow the lead of Oxford University Press by making room for Taylor among American writers. The hugely successful Houghton Mifflin and Norton anthologies gave Taylor a respectable place in the American canon and a broad audience. In the large American literature survey courses that dominated the fifties and sixties it would have been hard to find a student who did not recognize Taylor's most striking lines—"Who in this bowling alley bowled the sun?" and "Make me, O Lord, thy spinning-wheel complete!"

The first extended attempt to appraise Taylor's poetic enterprise after Grabo (1961) was William Sheick's *The Will and the Word: The Poetry of Edward Taylor* (1974). Stoutly within Miller's teachings regarding the Augustinian traditions of Taylor's New England, and also like Miller anticipating a growing transcendental theory that would lead in time to Jonathan Edwards and Ralph Waldo Emerson, Scheick emphasized Taylor's ideas concerning the continuities between God's goodness and human nature, even after the Fall. Where Grabo had stressed distinctions and separation, Scheick stressed Taylor's concept of the will as a mediating faculty between the earthly and divine, the mechanism that made possible the reciprocity between God and man. Reading both the sermons and poems through Augustine and Edwards, Scheick depicts a Taylor not quite so fallen in a Nature still good because it is yet God's handiwork. Scheick's Taylor is thus more naturalized, less mysticized, seeing the human will as the key faculty for opening the doors of the soul to divine love.

In Scheick's view, Taylor's language is a necessarily faulty bridge between mankind's clouded will and God's vitalizing love. Poetry is thus both a reaching out to God and a measuring of the self, the *Preparatory Meditations* functioning as "symbolic scriptures of the self." This concern with self-identity affiliates Taylor more with the American tradition than it does with the British metaphysical school. A year later Karl Keller strongly agreed that Taylor marked the beginning of a new American tradition, and had more in common with Edwards, Emerson, and Dickinson than with Donne and Herbert. Keller also shared Scheick's impatience with mysticism as a satisfactory model for Taylor's literary practice, but *The Example of Edward Taylor* (1975), much as it enhances our sense of how nature, the frontier, and Taylor's everyday life helped to shape his writing, is not content to naturalize

mystical experience or to make communion a substitute for union.
Keller suggested that Taylor is, as part of his *imitatio Christi,* an imitation saint, an impersonator, a pretender to achieved union, concerned
with the process rather than with the being—and thereby a poet rather
than a genuine mystic caught silently in the rictus of religious ecstasy.
There is considerable merit to this view.

There is also merit in other of Keller's particular arguments—that
Taylor's commitment to poetry constituted him a classical humanist as
well as a Christian one, that much of the energy of his verse comes from
the honesty with which he interprets the scatalogical implications of his
fallen state, and that the shocking simplicity of Taylor's verbal effects
have much in common with the distorting perspectives of American
primitive painting. These are all ingenious and captivating arguments,
whether one wishes to honor Keller's conclusions or not. Keller is less
valuable on the subject of Taylor's prose, though he uses it extensively,
and his treatment of *God's Determinations* is surprisingly unproductive,
but on most issues Keller's judgment compels agreement. His main
point—that it is not enough to use Taylor's poetry as a pool from which
to distill new ideas about Puritanism, but that all the Taylor that we
have must be used to appreciate the poet in him—that main point
Keller made vivaciously and powerfully. Impressively informed in the
growing mass of Taylor criticism, and possessed of the entire known
corpus of Taylor's work, Keller bristled with insights into every level of
Taylor's performance. By charging his study with an energy and gaiety
uncommon in Puritan studies, Keller's *Example* presented Taylor as a
vigorous and worthy artist in all his complex and rough-hewn texture.

But the main line of critical appreciation followed a different line.
Put most broadly, it sought both explanation and appreciation for
Taylor in his use of biblical materials and techniques. The Bible as the
great treasury or storehouse of poetic materials had never been entirely
ignored in Taylor criticism, but Peter Nicolaisen's 1966 monograph,
Die Bildlichkeit in der Dichtung Edward Taylors was the first study to
demonstrate extensively the biblical sources of Taylor's imagery, the
importance of typological interpretation, and the reliance upon biblical
rhetorical conventions—particularly the techniques of *amplificatio*—in
Taylor's verse. Nicolaisen was also among the first to appreciate what
Charles W. Mignon would call Taylor's "Decorum of Imperfection"—
the studied failure of Taylor's poetic strategy. But it was another German scholar, Ursula Brumm of Berlin, who recognized the centrality in
Taylor's work of biblical typology. She caught the attention of Ameri-

can scholars with her sweeping *Die Religiöse Typologie im amerikanischen Denken* (Leiden: E.J. Brill, 1963). There she placed Taylor near the beginning of a line of religious typologists in American literary symbolism—a line running from Samuel and Cotton Mather to Jonathan Edwards, Nathaniel Hawthorne, and Herman Melville. When Brumm's work was translated as *American Thought and Religious Typology* in 1970, she caught the quickening interest in typological symbolism at its height. For that was the same year the journal *Early American Literature* focused attention on typology as a mode of literary as well as biblical symbolism; the bulk of its essays were subsequently reprinted by Sacvan Bercovitch in *Typology and Early American Literature* (1972).

Edward Taylor had by this time emerged as a serious object of international inquiry into American literature: Nicolaisen and Brumm in Germany, Akiyama in Japan, Lal Sharma in connection with Persian poetry, Lalli in Italy—all expanded the relevant contexts by which Taylor might be more clearly perceived. Native historians of American poetry—Pearce, Waggoner, Gelpi—made serious room for him,[5] and he became the presiding spirit as well as the major subject of Robert Daly's study of early American aesthetics and symbolism, *God's Altar: The World and the Flesh* (1978)—having made possible a view of the function of symbolism and metaphor in seventeenth-century American Puritanism that had been previously unsuspected.

Considering Taylor's growing stature and recognition by the end of the seventies, it is somewhat surprising that the two most recent large treatments of him essentially ignore his place in a future American tradition, but seek to illuminate him by the light of Anglo-European traditions. By 1979, when Barbara K. Lewalski's *Protestant Poetics and the Seventeenth-Century Religious Lyric* appeared, Taylor's long-noted relationship with the metaphysical poets seemed an exhausted vein of exploration. But Lewalski was not interested in poets as members of a school identified by its technical mannerisms; what intrigued her was the fact that the seventeenth century produced the fullest flowering of devotional poetry in English. The great lyricists were all Protestant—John Donne, George Herbert, Henry Vaughan, Thomas Traherne, and with them, different but equal, Edward Taylor—and it is their Protestant heritage that Lewalski sees as definingly characteristic of their high art.

Chiefly that heritage centered on the Bible, which Protestant scholars in the Renaissance saw repeatedly as a compendium of literary kinds, an aesthetic, and a justification for devotional poetry, theories of metaphor and symbol, a philosophy of language, and an invitation if not a moral imperative to imitate. Little need for poets drenched in the Bible to seek their poetics in classical or even Catholic traditions. Major Pauline lyric forms—psalms, hymns, and spiritual songs—along with a dense poetic texture and a controlling typological symbology were immediate gifts of the scriptures. But the Bible offered ancillary genres as well—meditations, emblems, even sermons—all models for study, appreciation, and imitation. Lewalski explored the Protestant literature devoted to these matters in the sixteenth and seventeenth centuries with great learning, painstaking thoroughness, and authority. What emerged was a deep and fertile intellectual mulch out of which flowered the very different lyric expressions of her five major lyricists.

In Taylor Lewalski saw the end of this great tradition, examining him at careful length in her emphatic last chapter. She noted his greater-than-ordinary reliance upon emblems and types, as well as his peculiar adaptations of meditative procedures. And she noted, perhaps even more emphatically than had Keller and others, the centrality of failure in Taylor's devotional enterprise, giving greater emphasis to Taylor's conscious enactments of failure. Every strained rhyme and hobbled meter, each clumsy poem, confesses both the poet's desire and the soul's need. Each failing testifies to a power and grace beyond unaided human reach, and by doing so does in fact succeed in celebrating God's glory. By both confessing and demonstrating the impossible, Taylor in some sense achieves it.

Like Lewalski, Karen E. Rowe is little interested in earlier labels such as "Metaphysical" or "Baroque," and even less concerned with American traditions that may have derived from Taylor. In *Saint and Singer: Edward Taylor's Typology and the Poetics of Meditation* (1986), Rowe explores in the greatest detail to date the functions of typology in Taylor's thought and work. The result is a dense and powerful analysis both of the Protestant traditions of typological exegesis and of Taylor's debt to those traditions. By making typology the central feature of Taylor's thought, Rowe reenforces the striking unity of Taylor's mind.

Biblical typologists were concerned to show that New Testament phenomena fulfilled the promises and prophecies of the Old Testament, thereby containing all the laws and ceremonies, offices and personages, of the Old Testament somehow within itself. Thus Jesus as the Christ contains and transmutes on a spiritual plane the hope of Adam, the leadership of Abraham, the sufferings of Job, the heroic sacrifice of Samson, the holy singing of David. Historically speaking, Jesus imitates these predecessors; but considered providentially, Christ precedes history, and so the historical figures are said to be types of Christ by anticipatory imitation, and Christ is then called the antitype. This reliance upon figural imitation distinguishes typology from other modes of symbolic or metaphorical relationship. Rowe calls typology "a mode of spiritual perception" that resembles a literary mode, but is not itself simply literary or rhetorical.[6]

Typology is thus an *imitatio figura* parallel to Taylor's dear *imitatio Christi*. The Bible exists as two mutually reflecting looking glasses, Old and New Testaments sharing a single truth. Moreover, when Taylor looks into that combined looking glass, he hopes to see mirrored there his own soul. He would be the willing sacrifice, the enduring Job, the heroic Samson, the musical David—and so he would clothe himself in the wedding garment that is Christ, and become identical with the antitype.[7] Rowe distinguishes Taylor's devotional typology from the kind of recapitulative typology described in Sacvan Bercovitch's *The Puritan Origins of the American Self* (1973) and Mason Lowance's *The Language of Canaan* (1980), both of which show the ways in which later American writing and social behavior are valorized by traditional comparisons to scriptural models. Unlike his friend Cotton Mather, Taylor foregoes justifying the politics of his own day by calling upon the models of Moses or Nehemiah; not every fancied similitude constitutes a valid typological reading.

What did constitute legitimate devotional typology had been hammered out by numerous writers before Taylor, who used them freely and openly, particularly Thomas Taylor, in *Christ Revealed; or the Old Testament Explained* (1635) and Samuel Mather, in *Figures or Types of the Old Testament by which Christ and the Heavenly Things of the Gospel were Preached and Shadowed to the People of God of Old* (1683). Rowe shows in detail Taylor's reliance upon both the system of types and the particular interpretations offered by these two writers, as well as the ways in which Taylor combined and moved beyond them in his invention of poetic metaphors. Rowe hereby enables us to appreciate Taylor's typology as something more than one poetic technique among many shared with the other devotional lyricists of the seventeenth century, but as an essential spiritual commitment of Taylor's, a blueprint for the bridge between the mundane and the eternal, the doctrinal and the poetic, that Mignon and Scheick and Keller and many others knew existed but had not yet displayed so thoroughly.

Rowe rightly maintains that typology is not merely a technique, but a pervasive consciousness, crucial both to Taylor's public ministry and to his private poetry. It is not a random collection of ingenious comparisons, but an elaborate system of apparently necessary, and therefore strangely logical, connections. But its character is less logical than intuitive, the singular, instantaneous, time-free awareness of identities—perhaps better represented by Ramist diagrams of agreements than by Aristotelian arguments. We might think of typology, then, as like a system of superimposed transparencies, each in itself complete, yet when perceived simultaneously, constituting a whole richer and truer than any of its layered parts, though each layer is itself both consummately rich and true. Thus—to choose the example most important to Taylor—the lowest transparency might be the Old Testament conception of the Feast of the Passover, replete in its own religious and historical significance. The New Testament overlays that with the ceremony of the Lord's Supper, matching in all respects except its deeper spiritual colors. Atop that lay the mundane duty of the Christian minister to administer the commemorative sacrament of the eucharist, and on top of all these lay the richest transparency—the celebratory feast of the marriage of God to His favored creatures. Rightly—spiritually—perceived, each feast typifies the others, all properly centered in the redemptive incarnation of Christ. All layers manifest a single truth, though each retains its particular differences, telescoping or collapsing time into eternal presence.

This retention of the individual layers of significance within an overriding unity enables Rowe to demonstrate a progressive connection between Taylor's doctrinal and his aesthetic activities. Working with the unparalleled advantage of access to the yet unpublished homilies of *Upon the Types of the Old Testament,* Rowe shows the vigorous presence of typological understandings at work in his Foundation Day Sermon and its revision as *A Particular Church,* in his "Christomimetic" *Christographia,* in the somewhat politicized reactions to Solomon Stoddard of his *Treatise Concerning the Lord's Supper* and other anti-Stoddardean compositions, and finally in the unified progress of the *Preparatory Meditations* from painful preparation to ecstatic celebration.

Rowe benefits in two ways by putting typology at the heart of Taylor's thought and poetry. First she is enabled to appreciate the art with which Taylor extrapolates from established typological traditions. Poems that seemed before dully doctrinal and forced can now be shown to be ingenious elaborations of underlying, submerged, subliminal systems of analysis. Her readings of *Preparatory Meditations* 2.27 and 2.61 offer beautiful displays of Taylor's virtuosity. What is more,

Taylor's apparently wild leaps from one metaphor to another, which create what I have called surrealistic effects and which have bothered critics since their first exposure, now look like reasonable, if recondite, elaborations on a very explicit system of relationships, a system, fortunately, whose complexity resists easy reductions.

Secondly, Rowe uses typology to demonstrate a relatively uniform development over the long course of Taylor's career. That in turn permits us to see a coherence in the *Meditations* that has been claimed before, but never shown so explicitly or successfully. Even at the beginning, when the *Meditations* may be seen to be primarily preparatory for Westfield sacrament Sundays, their typology looks forward to an eschatalogical vision, the union of Christ and his Church in glory. But as Taylor ages, as he comes nearer the eschatalogical realization himself, as his ardor for the ultimate union intensifies, he moves with increasingly exclusivity to meditations upon Canticles. Read thus, the entire sequence is personally autobiographical, and stands as the record of one soul's progress towards bliss.

Where Rowe sees Taylor's use of personal pronouns as translations from the communal soul to Taylor's individual autobiographical self, I have argued for translation in precisely the opposite direction—that Taylor has converted personal desire and frustration into a representative saintly speaker who must perforce experience what Taylor in personal fact cannot. Taylor still seems to me to create in the *Preparatory Meditations* a speaker who defines and measures himself against a mystical pattern that he can admire, approach, and use, even if he can never realize the mystical ecstasy in person. Unlike Scheick and Keller, Rowe does not so much reject this reading as she offers another—the typological reading that remains within Taylor's everyday experience while still permitting the "realms of visions" that I have called mystical.

Saint and Singer—itself the fruit of long gestation—is handsome evidence of the quality of Taylor scholarship and critical appraisal written this past quarter-century. Critical sophistication in colonial literary studies and our appreciation of Taylor have flowered simultaneously and not coincidentally. When Mignon's edition of *Upon the Types* becomes generally available, it will no doubt yield new perceptions to new eyes. So *Saint and Singer,* the culmination of one phase of Taylor studies, must itself become but as a stepping stone for others to use to go beyond it.

Moreover, Rowe ends her fine study with at once the most important and most vulnerable observations. Her Taylor is not content with preparatory meditation, nor with celebration of the Lord's Supper, nor even with his imagined and ardently hoped-for seating among the wedding guests at the banquet of saints. He will be the holy singer, the psalmist, the hymnist at the eternal feast. No longer tongue-tied and snick-snarled, with a sharp quill on smooth paper, and with blotless ink of radiant clarity, he will be the voice of Divinity—the Milton, Dante, Augustine, David, Solomon, and Moses. But this says at the same time that Taylor the poet of a particular time and place can neither be understood nor appreciated without access to very recondite systems of significance and value. Rowe's typology and Lewalski's emblems make visible the intricacies of a special aesthetic, appreciation of which turns dull poems into shining feats of imaginative brilliance, and good poems into even better ones. Fortunately that aesthetic has been recoverable, but the need to recover it suggests how remote, how long gone, those principles of poetic construction are, and how much the durability of Taylor's accomplishment depends upon its accidental congruence with later aesthetics and later poetics. For by reconstructing the bridges that turn doctrine and devotional experience into metaphor and verse, such criticism diminishes the qualities of shock and surprise that have been from the beginning so much the measure of our delight in Taylor's poetry.

The question of genuine accessibility—especially to the *Preparatory Meditations*—deserves more serious consideration, especially in the light of recent judgments regarding the devotional poems and commentaries of Saint John of the Cross. Jane Ackerman speculates subtly that works such as the *Living Flame of Love* escape literary canons altogether, being the creatures of and property of the Carmelite monastic practices that alone can nurture and understand them.[8] Out of the monastery, like Emerson's seashells, their glory and shine fade into pale reminders, relics only. Clearly Taylor's meditations escape that degree of privacy, but the comparison is instructive.

So too might be a closer look at another Spanish poet, the Mexican nun Sor Juana Inés de la Cruz, whose work appeared in Madrid in the 1690s. A. Owen Aldridge made a solid beginning in this direction in his comparatist study of *Early American Literature* (1982), although he is more interested in Taylor's baroque techniques than he is in the spiritual and devotional inspiration shared by both Taylor and Sor Juana. Scholars with broad comparatist interests—Harold S. Jantz and Austin Warren, for example[9]—seem more alert to and more comfortable with the baroque character of Taylor's taste than do strict Americanists.

With an aesthetic that uses bewilderingly intricate devices to release powerful emotional, sometimes spiritual, surges, the baroque mentality has too much in common with both emblematic and typological modes of thought to continue to be slighted in Taylor studies, whether we take our hints from architecture, painting, or music.

Odd to see where material and objective scholarship brings us. The editing and transcribing, the footnoting and doctrinal analyses, the insistent gathering of meaningful contexts and the intricacies of ecclesiastical polity—all establish Taylor within a mosaic of unexpected connections, including comparison with a Mexican nun who flamed into brief glory with three volumes of poems. They called her "la decima musa," just as forty years earlier in colonial New England Anne Bradstreet had been announced to the world of English poetry as another Sappho, a Tenth Muse. The comparison with Sor Juana is not as far-fetched as it seems at first glance, for her work looks boldly in two directions—in one towards Luis de Góngora, whose technical virtuosity entertained and fascinated readers of the Golden Age and contributed to the mannerism of the English metaphysicals; in another towards the elements of Aztec poetry and culture that underlay Mexican Christianity in the seventeenth century. Her poetry reached to the image-intensive, pagan, even archetypal patterns that reflected, if not an equality of the Sacred Heart of Jesus with the ripped-out sacrificial hearts of Tenochtitlan, certainly the proximity of Aztec worship of sun and corn with Christian worship of Son and bread. Of course Sor Juana saw these as opposed principles; it matters almost as much that she placed them proximately, sensed their affinities, because it is their likeness that she hoped would make a common path for false-worshipping Indians and followers of the true faith.[10]

In a parallel manner new worlds and old meet in Edward Taylor's temple of art or entempled heart. In northern Mexico during the seventeenth century substantial adobe churches were erected, thick-walled, squat, thrust massively out of the earth from which the adobe came, and constantly pressing down to return to that dust, emblems of mortality. But inside they were sometimes afire with color, gilt, and glory, a feast of busy delights, swirling and florid arabesques of devotion, achieving in paint and plaster the soaring effects of Spanish cathedrals, without gold, silver, or precious jewels. Outside, fate; inside, aspiration. That same effect shows in the Quebec of Taylor's century—dark, formidable, stone exteriors enclosing as much light as paint and candles and delicately carved wood allow. One supposes, on these colonial models, the nature of Taylor's temple—clapboards and shingles, plain deal furnishings, an exterior very like that of the Westfield meeting-house, with a prospect of eternity.

Thomas Hooker, speaking about meditation, offers a nice analogy for the ongoing appraisal of this real heart property: "a present apprehension peeps in as it were through the crevis or key-hole, looks in at the window as a man passeth by: but Meditation lifts up the latch and goes into each room, pries into every corner of the house, and surveyes the composition and making of it, with all the blemishes in it."[11] Perry Miller, we might say, gave us the survey, the plans, some fine exterior sketches, the principles of construction, and some glimpses through the keyhole. But it has been a host of others—Scheick, Brumm, Keller, Mignon, the Davises, Lewalski, and Rowe among the most prominent—who have rubbed off the grime of ages, removing the overlays of Victorian wallpaper and Enlightenment whitewash to restore the riotous interior of the Puritan heart. They have shown us how the simple and austere exterior of a grim and prim institution housed worlds elsewhere. Through the *pentimenti* of their analyses we trace in Taylor's extravagant images the persistent force of the mortal imagination to be rendered eternal, raised out of the accents of Mexico and Quebec, or even Westfield, founded deeper than London or Paris, Geneva or Little Gidding, reaching back beyond Rome and Constantinople through the Tertullians and Origens and Jeromes upon whom Taylor so insatiably fed, past the Gospels and the Gentiles, past even David to the Middle Eastern world—intricate, ornate, gorgeous, Oriental—not to the hirsute prophets of the desert, but to the ardent spiritual grandeur of Solomon's Song of Songs.

Notes and References

Chapter One

1. John Hoyt Lockwood, *Westfield and Its Historic Influences* (Springfield, Mass.: Press of Springfield Printing and Binding Co., 1922), 1:138.

2. Actually there is no hard evidence for the family tradition that Taylor forbade publication of any of his writings. But see Kenneth B. Murdock, *Literature and Theology in Colonial New England* (Cambridge, Mass.: Harvard University Press, 1949), 167; Quinn, Murdock, et al., *The Literature of the American People* (New York: Appleton-Century-Crofts, Inc., 1951), 57; Perry Miller, *The American Puritans: Their Prose and Poetry* (New York: Peter Smith, Inc., 1956), 301; and *The New England Mind: From Colony to Province* (Cambridge, Mass.: Harvard University Press, 1953), 31; and Richard D. Altick, *The Scholar Adventurers* (New York: Macmillan, 1950), 307.

3. Taylor's birth date has been estimated anywhere from 1642 to 1645. 1642 raises several problems, but Donald E. Stanford establishes this date with authority in *The Poems of Edward Taylor* (New Haven, Conn.: Yale University Press, 1960), xxxix. The description of Taylor's conversion is from Taylor's "Relation" (1679) in the "Public Records of the Church at Westfield," in Thomas M. and Virginia L. Davis, editors, *Unpublished Writings of Edward Taylor* (Boston: Twayne, 1981), 1:97–104 (subsequently referred to as *UW*).

4. William T. Costello, S. J., *The Scholastic Curriculum at Early Seventeenth-Century Cambridge* (Cambridge, Mass.: Harvard University Press, 1958), 147. Costello's analysis of a college disputation (19–25) illuminates Taylor's later practice.

5. Without the benefit of Taylor's sermons, Walter J. Ong simply erred in the opinion that "Edward Taylor . . . is the least Puritan and least Ramist of all New England writers," *Ramus: Method and the Decay of Dialogue from the Art of Discourse to the Art of Reason* (Cambridge, Mass.: Harvard University Press, 1958), 287. See also Leon Howard, "Renaissance Uses of Ramean Logic," in *Essays on Puritans and Puritanism* (Albuquerque: University of New Mexico Press, 1986), 135–203.

6. Ong, *Ramus,* 12 *et passim*; Costello, *Scholastic Curriculum,* 33,146; Samuel Eliot Morison, *Harvard College in the Seventeenth Century* (Cambridge, Mass.: Harvard University Press, 1936), 1:165; Norman Fiering, *Moral Philosophy at Seventeenth-Century Harvard: A Discipline in Transition* (Chapel Hill: University of North Carolina Press, 1981).

7. *Diary of Edward Taylor,* edited by Francis Murphy (Springfield, Mass.: Connecticut Valley Historical Museum, 1964), 29.

8. Thomas H. Johnson, *The Poetical Works of Edward Taylor* (New York: Rockland Editions, 1939), 11–12.

9. *Diary,* 37.

10. Lockwood, *Westfield,* 1:151.

11. See the letter urging Increase Mather to assist the publication of Daniel Denton's "A Divine Soliloquy," *Collections of the Massachusetts Historical Society,* 4th ser. 8 (1868): 629–31.

12. Johnson lists these volumes by title, *Poetical Works,* 201–20.

13. Item 22 of the Taylor commonplace book in the possession of the Massachusetts Historical Society.

14. Ibid., Items 2 and 3.

15. Ibid., Item 5.

16. William B. Goodman, "Edward Taylor Writes His Love," *New England Quarterly* 27 (December 1954): 510–15.

17. Davis and Davis, *UW,* 3:42–3.

18. "Public Records of the Church," *UW* 1:4; Lockwood, *Westfield,* 1:218.

19. *UW* 1:8.

20. Ibid., 10–96.

21. Ibid., 160.

22. Samuel Sewall records hearing Taylor preach excellently at the Old South Church "upon short warning." "The Letter Book of Samuel Sewall," *Collections of the Massachusetts Historical Society,* 6th ser. 2 (1886–88): 274.

23. *Collections of the Massachusetts Historical Society,* 4th ser. 8 (1868): 629–31. See also Item 3 in "China's Description," a commonplace book in the Yale University Library.

24. Meditation 2.110.

25. Miller, *From Colony to Province,* 227. But see *UW* 2:1–13.

26. Solomon Stoddard, *An Appeal to the Learned . . . Against the Exceptions of Mr. Mather* (Boston, 1709), 70. Taylor's argument and the entire controversy is treated most authoritatively in *UW* 2.

27. Solomon Stoddard, *The Doctrine of Instituted Churches Explained and Proved from the Word of God* (London, 1700), 27.

28. Williston Walker says the proceedings "awakened no debate of consequence," *A History of the Congregational Churches in the United States* (New York: Charles Scribner's Sons, 1894), 189–90.

29. Miller, *From Colony to Province,* 232.

30. The complete correspondence appears in *UW* 2:63–66.

31. These are printed as *Edward Taylor's Treatise Concerning the Lord's Supper,* edited by Norman S. Grabo (East Lansing: Michigan State University Press, 1966), 126. Subsequent references are to *TCLS.*

32. Stoddard, *An Appeal,* 53.

33. Anonymous, *An Appeal, of Some of the Unlearned, both to the Learned and Unlearned* (Boston, 1709), 28.

34. John L. Sibley, *Biographical Sketches of Graduates of Harvard University* (Boston: Charles William Sever, University Bookstore, 1881), 5:342–43.
35. *UW* 1:430–34.
36. Henry W. Taylor, "Edward Taylor," in William B. Sprague, *Annals of the American Pulpit* (New York: Harper & Brothers, 1857), 1: 178.

Chapter Two

1. Evelyn Underhill, *Mysticism: A Study in the Nature and Development of Man's Spiritual Consciousness* (New York: Meridian Books, 1955), xiv. First published in 1910, Underhill remains the best synthetic analysis of Christian mystical traditions.
2. *UW* 1: 98.
3. Ibid., 97.
4. Jonathan Edwards, "Personal Narrative," *Jonathan Edwards: Representative Selections,* edited by Clarence H. Faust and Thomas H. Johnson, rev. ed. (New York: Hill and Wang, Inc., 1962), 60–61.
5. Underhill's term.
6. William Ralph Inge, *Christian Mysticism* (New York: Meridian Books, 1956), 156–59.
7. This is a continuation of the practice popular among Renaissance neo-Platonists from Ficino to Taylor's contemporaries, the Cambridge Platonists.
8. *Edward Taylor's Christographia,* edited by Norman S. Grabo (New Haven, Conn.: Yale University Press, 1962), 131, 122. Subsequent citations are to *C.*
9. 1 Cor. 1: 19–27.
10. H. M. Margoliouth, editor, *Thomas Traherne: Centuries, Poems, and Thanksgivings* (Oxford: Oxford University Press, 1958), I: iv: 3, 169.
11. The fifth poem in *God's Determinations* is entitled "God's Selecting Love in the Decree." Stanford, 399.
12. Ibid., 11. 23–24.
13. The best discussions of this ecclesiastical problem are in Perry Miller, "The Marrow of Puritan Divinity," in *Errand into the Wilderness* (Cambridge, Mass.: Harvard University Press, 1956), 48–98; in chapters 12 and 15 of his *The New England Mind: The Seventeenth Century* (Cambridge, Mass.: Harvard University Press, 1939); and his *From Colony to Province* (Cambridge, Mass.: Harvard University Press, 1953) 68–118, 210–47. Theological aspects are emphasized in Peter Y. De Jong, *The Covenant Idea in New England Theology, 1620–1847* (Grand Rapids, Mich.: Wm. B. Eerdmans Publishing Company, 1945). The importance of verbal signs and testimony is discussed in my introduction to *TCLS,* xxxii–xliii.
14. Cited in Inge, *Christian Mysticism,* 23.
15. Underhill, *Mysticism,* 204.

16. The full title of this work points up this struggle: *God's Determinations Touching His Elect: and the Elect's Combat in their Conversion and Coming up to God in Christ, together with the Comfortable Effects Thereof.*

17. S. Foster Damon, review of "The Poetical Works of Edward Taylor," *New England Quarterly* 12 (December 1939): 780.

18. John Calvin, *Institutes of the Christian Religion,* edited and translated by John Allen, 7th ed., rev. (Philadelphia, n.d.), bk 2, chap. 1, para. 8.

19. Ibid., para. 7.

20. *C,* 10–15. Miller points out that two theories prevailed about this matter in New England; Taylor followed Augustine and Calvin rather than his New England colleagues. See Miller, *Jonathan Edwards* (New York: Sloane, 1949), 277.

21. Ola E. Winslow, *Meetinghouse Hill: 1630–1783* (New York: Norton, 1952), 31–49.

22. Underhill, *Mysticism,* 222–27.

23. Ibid., p. 310 ff.

24. Louis L. Martz, *The Poetry of Meditation* (New Haven, Conn.: Yale University Press, 1954), 14–15.

25. Underhill, *Mysticism,* 46.

26. Martz, *Poetry of Meditation,* 16.

27. See above, p. 11.

28. Martz, *Poetry of Meditation,* 154.

29. Richard Baxter, *The Saints Everlasting Rest: or, a Treatise of the Blessed State of the Saints in their enjoyment of God in Glory. Wherein is showed its Excellency and Certainty; the Misery of those that lose it, the way to Attain it, and assurance of it; and how to live in the continual delightful Foretastes of it, by the help of Meditation.* . . . (London, 1649 [1650]), 691–92.

30. Ibid., 662.

31. Ibid., 719.

32. Ibid., 662.

33. Ibid., 749–51.

34. Martz, *Poetry of Meditation,* 174. But Catholic devotional books gave the same advice much earlier. Translations of two books by Luis de Granados—*An Excellent Treatise of Consideration and Prayer* (p. 6), bound with *Of Prayer and Meditation* (London, 1592), sig. 1₉v—clearly indicate the affinity of the meditation with the sermon. And Gaspar Loarte's *The Exercise of a Christian Life* (Paris, 1579), which Baxter made a main cause of his own conversion, established the same relationship, p. 66.

35. Increase Mather, *Practical Truths Tending to Promote the Power of Godliness* (Boston, 1682), 79.

36. Ibid., 135.

37. The full subtitle to the *Christographia* is "A Discourse touching Christ's Person, Natures, the Personal Union of the Natures, Qualifications,

and Operations Opened, Confirmed, and Practically Improved in Several Sermons Delivered upon Certain Sacrament Days unto the Church and People of God in Westfield."

38. Underhill, *Mysticism*, 240; Inge, *Christian Mysticism*, 16.

39. R. C. Zaehner, *Mysticism Sacred and Profane: An Inquiry into Some Varieties of Preternatural Experience* (Oxford: Oxford University Press, 1957), 32.

40. Inge, *Christian Mysticism*, 17.

41. Henry Vaughan, "The World," *The Works of Henry Vaughan*, edited by L. C. Martin, 2d ed. (Oxford: Oxford University Press, 1957), 466.

42. Louis L. Martz, "Foreword," *The Poems of Edward Taylor*, edited by Donald E. Stanford (New Haven, Conn.: Yale University Press, 1960), xxxii.

43. Underhill, *Mysticism*, 288.

44. Increase Mather, *The Mystery of Christ opened and applyed in Several Sermons, Concerning the Persons, Offices, and Glory of Jesus Christ* (Boston, 1685), 88–89.

45. Ibid., 98.

46. Ibid., 110.

47. John Milton, "Paradise Lost," 1: 36–40.

48. Underhill, *Mysticism*, 415.

49. Ibid., 425.

50. Ibid., 136–37.

51. *Preparatory Meditations* 2.115–53.

52. Underhill, *Mysticism*, 137.

53. Ibid., 173; Zaehner, *Mysticism Sacred and Profane*, 187 f.

54. Inge, *Christian Mysticism*, 33, 191.

Chapter Three

1. Most preachers emphasized the application rather than the doctrinal proof. See Babette May Levy, *Preaching in the First Half Century of New England History*, in *Studies in Church History* 6 (Hartford, Conn., 1945), 94.

2. *C,* xxx–xliii.

3. For the creators themselves, see Brewster Ghiselin, *The Creative Process: A Symposium* (New York: Mentor Books, 1952); for the sociologist, Robert N. Wilson, *Man Made Plain: The Poet in Contemporary Society* (Cleveland: Howard Allen Inc., 1958); and for the philosopher, Susanne K. Langer, *Feeling and Form* (New York: Macmillan, 1957). Also see Underhill, *Mysticism*, 74–80.

4. Samuel Taylor Coleridge, *Biographia Literaria: or, Biographical Sketches of My Literary Life and Opinions*, edited by J. Shawcross (Oxford: Oxford University Press, 1907), 1, chapter 13, 202.

5. Miller, *Seventeenth Century*, 360.

6. *UW,* 3:4.

7. Ibid., 24–30.

8. William Butler Yeats, "The Symbolism of Poetry," *Ideas of Good and Evil* (London: Bullen, 1903), 242.

9. Compare stanza 9 of "Contemplations" with Taylor's *PM* 1.22:

> But shall the bird sing forth thy praise, and shall
> The little bee present her thankful hum?
> But I who see thy shining glory fall
> Before mine eyes, stand blockish, dull, and dumb?

10. Richard Baxter, *Poetical Fragments: Heart-Imployment with God and It Self,* 3d ed. (London, 1699), sigs. A_4r and A_3r.

11. Thomas H. Johnson, "Colonial Voice Reheard in Verse," *Saturday Review,* 6 August 1960, 12.

Chapter Four

1. *Graven Images: New England Stonecarving and Its Symbols, 1650–1815* (Middletown, Conn.: Wesleyan University Press, 1966).

2. See John Bierhorst, editor, *Four Masterworks of American Indian Literature* (New York: Farrar, Straus and Giroux, 1974), 107–83.

3. *UW* 3:116–23.

4. An excellent study of the Puritan elegy is Robert Henson's "Sorry After a Godly Manner" (unpublished diss., UCLA, 1957). See also Robert Daly, *God's Altar: The World and the Flesh in Puritan Poetry* (Berkeley: University of California Press, 1978), 162–70, and Kenneth B. Murdock, *Handkerchiefs from Paul* (Cambridge, Mass.: Harvard University Press, 1927).

5. *UW* 3:40–41.

6. Ibid., 111.

7. Ibid., 106–07.

8. Malcolm Mackenzie Ross, *Poetry and Dogma* (New Brunswick, N.J.: Octagon, 1954), 152, 182, and passim.

9. See above, 37.

10. Philip Pain, *Daily Meditations,* edited by Leon Howard (San Marino, California: Henry E. Huntington Library and Art Gallery, 1936).

11. In Stanford, *Poems,* xxiii.

12. Ibid., xxi.

13. Levy, *Preaching in the First Half Century,* 89.

14. In Stanford, *Poems,* xxiii.

15. Austin Warren, "Edward Taylor's Poetry: Colonial Baroque," *Kenyon Review* 3 (Summer 1941): 366.

16. William R. Manierre, II, "Verbal Patterns in the Poetry of Edward Taylor," *College English* 23 (1962): 296–99.

17. George Puttenham, *The Art of English Poesie* (1589), ed. Edward Arber, *English Reprints* 7 (London, 1869), 211.

18. Samuel Johnson, "Life of Cowley," *Lives of the English Poets*, vol. 1 (London: J. M. Dent & Sons Ltd, 1925), 39.

19. John Weemes, *The Christian Synagogue*, 4th ed. (London, 1633), 285–87.

20. Cited in Martz, *Poetry of Meditation*, 257.

21. Joseph Hall, "The Art of Divine Meditation," *The Works of the Right Reverend Joseph Hall, D. D. Bishop of Exeter and Afterwards of Norwich*, edited by Philip Wynter, rev. ed. (Oxford, 1863), 6:50.

22. Baxter, *Saints Everlasting Rest*, 678.

23. As in his "Upon a Spider Catching a Fly." Certainly a nature poem in one sense, Taylor is less interested in the insects than in the moral they allegorize: "Strive not above what strength hath got."

24. See above, 57–70.

25. Underhill, *Mysticism*, 141–46.

26. Inge, *Christian Mysticism*, 220–21.

27. Rosemary Freeman, *English Emblem Books* (London: Chatto and Windus, 1948), 238–39. The fullest application of emblem materials to English devotional poets of this period is Barbara Kiefer Lewalski's *Protestant Poetics and the Seventeenth-Century Religious Lyric* (Princeton, N.J.: Princeton University Press, 1979).

28. Ibid., 116.

29. Francis Quarles, *Emblemes*, V, iii, 11. 25–30, in Alexander B. Grosart, editor, *The Complete Works in Prose and Verse* (Edinburgh: T. and A. Constable, 1881), 3:91.

30. Freeman, *English Emblem Books*, 117.

31. Ibid., 173–203.

32. Ibid., 47–52.

33. Ibid., facing p. 33.

34. Quarles, *Emblemes*, III, xi. in *Works*, 75.

35. See Martz's analysis of Meditation 1.29, in Stanford, *Poems*, xxxii–xxxiv, and of the typological poems, Meditations 2.1–30.

36. Austin Warren, *Rage for Order* (Ann Arbor: University of Michigan Press, 1948), 17.

37. Typological systems offer another way of accounting for the apparent illogicality of such poetic imagery. See both Lewalski and Karen E. Rowe, *Saint and Singer: Edward Taylor's Typology and the Poetics of Meditation* (Cambridge: Cambridge University Press, 1986).

38. Martz, in Stanford, *Poems*, xiii, and Johnson, 23.

39. Johnson includes the "Prologue" as the first poem of *God's Determinations*; Stanford—with greater warrant from its position in Taylor's manuscript—places it before the *Preparatory Meditations*.

40. Nathalia Wright, "The Morality Tradition in the Poetry of Edward Taylor," *American Literature* 18 (March 1946): 1–17.

Chapter Five

1. Ludwig, *Graven Images,* esp. 67–232, 234–36.

2. Larzer Ziff, *Puritanism in America: New Culture in a New World* (New York: The Viking Press, 1973), x.

3. Published by the Johns Hopkins University Press.

4. See Mignon, "The Nebraska Edward Taylor Manuscript: 'Upon the Types of the Old Testament,' " *Early American Literature* 12 (1977/78): 296–301, and "Christ the Glory of All Types: The Initial Sermon from Edward Taylor's 'Upon the Types of the Old Testament,' " *William and Mary Quarterly,* 3d ser., 37 (April 1980): 286–301.

5. Roy Harvey Pearce, *The Continuity of American Poetry* (Princeton, N.J.: Princeton University Press, 1961); Hyatt H. Waggoner, *American Poets from the Puritans to the Present* (Boston: Houghton Mifflin, 1968); and Albert Gelpi, *The Tenth Muse: The Psyche of the American Poet* (Cambridge, Mass.: Harvard University Press, 1975).

6. Karen E. Rowe, *Saint and Singer,* 140.

7. Ibid., 249.

8. Professor Ackerman addressed this problem in "The Feminine in Spanish Mystical Literature," Symposium on Mysticism and Scripture, University of Tulsa, 23–24 February 1987.

9. See Jantz's general treatment of the baroque in "The First Century of New England Verse," *Proceedings of the American Antiquarian Society,* n.s. 53 (October 1943): 219–508, and Warren's in *Rage for Order,* 1–18.

10. I take these images from Sor Juana's *Loa para el auto sacramental de "El divino Narciso,"* in *Obras completas de Sor Juana Inés de la Cruz,* edited by Alfonso Méndez Plancarte (Mexico: Fondo de Cultura Económica, 1955), 3: 3–21.

11. *The Application of Redemption* (1659), cited in Roy Harvey Pearce, editor, *Colonial American Writing,* 2d ed. (New York: Holt, Rinehart and Winston, Inc., 1969), 106.

Selected Bibliography

PRIMARY SOURCES

Taylor's major poems were first edited by Thomas H. Johnson, *The Poetical Works of Edward Taylor* (New York: Rockland Editions, 1939, reissued by Princeton University Press in 1943). Donald E. Stanford first published all the *Preparatory Meditations*, other major poems, and some minor ones in *The Poems of Edward Taylor* (New Haven: Yale University Press, 1960), which was abridged for a paperback edition in 1963. *Edward Taylor's Minor Poetry*, the third volume of *The Unpublished Writings of Edward Taylor*, edited by Thomas M. and Virginia L. Davis (Boston: Twayne, 1981) collects all the minor poetry, excepting the 21,500-line *Metrical History of Christianity*, published in typescript by Donald E. Stanford (Cleveland: Micro Photo, Inc., 1962).

Taylor's sermons appear in the following editions: *Edward Taylor's Christographia*, edited by Norman S. Grabo (New Haven: Yale University Press, 1962); *Edward Taylor's Treatise Concerning the Lord's Supper*, edited by Norman S. Grabo (East Lansing: Michigan State University Press, 1965); *Edward Taylor's "Church Records" and Related Sermons* appear as volume 1 of *Unpublished Writings*, edited by Davis and Davis; Charles W. Mignon's edition of thirty-six Sacrament-Day sermons called *Upon the Types of the Old Testament* is scheduled to appear from the University of Nebraska Press very soon. Francis X. Murphy has edited *The Diary of Edward Taylor* (Springfield, Mass.: Connecticut Valley Historical Museum, 1964). Taylor's contributions to the Stoddardean Controversy appear as *Edward Taylor vs. Solomon Stoddard: The Nature of the Lord's Supper*, the second volume of *Unpublished Writings*. Analysis of the contents of these works and information concerning unedited manuscripts can be found in Norman S. Grabo and Jana Wainwright, "Edward Taylor," in *Fifteen American Authors before 1900: Bibliographical Essays on Research and Criticism*, edited by Earl N. Harbert and Robert A. Rees, rev. ed. (Wisconsin: University of Wisconsin Press, 1984), 439–67.

SECONDARY SOURCES

Black, Mindele. "Edward Taylor: Heaven's Sugar Cake," *New England Quarterly* 29 (June 1956):159–81. A mature evaluation of Taylor's Calvinistic modification of his Catholic devotional tradition.

Brumm, Ursula. *American Thought and Religious Typology.* Translated by John Hoaglund. New Brunswick, N.J.: Rutgers University Press, 1970. One of the earliest and richest attempts to place Edward Taylor in an American typological tradition.

Colacurcio, Michael J. "God's Determinations Touching Half-Way Membership: Occasion and Audience in Edward Taylor," *American Literature* 39 (November 1967): 298–314. The social, ecclesiastical, and theological context for Taylor's most ambitious occasional work.

Daly, Robert. *God's Altar: The World and the Flesh in Puritan Poetry.* Berkeley: University of California Press, 1978. An important advance in American Puritan aesthetics, dictated largely by the example of Taylor.

Gelpi, Albert. *The Tenth Muse: The Psyche of the American Poet.* Cambridge: Harvard University Press, 1975. Places Taylor's radical experiments in language in the American typological tradition from Emerson to Ginsberg.

Grabo, Norman S. "Edward Taylor's Spiritual Huswifery," *PMLA* 79 (December 1964): 554–60. An extended reading of "Huswifery" as the culmination of Taylor's devotional, theological, and ecclesiastical principles.

Johnson, Thomas H., editor. *The Poetical Works of Edward Taylor.* New York: Rockland Editions, 1939; rpt. Princeton University Press, 1943. A brilliantly selected edition with general introduction and glossary; contains *God's Determinations,* thirty-one *Meditations,* five miscellaneous poems, and a very useful list of Taylor's library.

Keller, Karl. *The Example of Edward Taylor.* Amherst: The University of Massachusetts Press, 1975. Excellent and vigorous readings of many poems, placing Taylor in a New England artistic tradition stretching to Frost and Grandma Moses.

Lewalski, Barbara Kiefer. *Protestant Poetics and the Seventeenth-Century Religious Lyric.* Princeton: Princeton University Press, 1979. Replaces Taylor among "the major religious lyric poets of the century—Donne, Herbert, Vaughan, and Traherne."

Lockwood, John Hoyt. *Westfield and Its Historic Influences.* 2 vols. Springfield, Mass.: Press of Springfield Printing and Binding Co., 1922. Vol. 1 is the most complete record of the area in which Taylor lived and worked; excellent background.

Nicolaisen, Peter. *Die Bildlichkeit in der Dichtung Edward Taylors.* Neumunster: Karl Wachholtz, 1966: On Taylor's use of Bible-drawn images of amplification.

Pearce, Roy Harvey. *The Continuity of American Poetry.* Princeton: Princeton University Press, 1961. Incorporates Pearce's 1950 judgment that Taylor must be evaluated within the limitations imposed upon him by his colonial culture.

Rowe, Karen E. *Saint and Singer: Edward Taylor's Typology and the Poetics of*

Tradition. Cambridge: Cambridge University Press, 1986. Thorough examination of Taylor's uses of typological traditions; detailed use of *Upon the Types.*

Russell, Gene. *A Concordance to the Poems of Edward Taylor.* Washington, D.C.: Microcard Editions 24 (1973). A computer-generated concordance based on Stanford's edition of *Poems.*

Scheick, William J. *The Will and the Word: The Poetry of Edward Taylor.* Athens: The University of Georgia Press, 1974. Metaphor and desire as parallel intermediaries in Taylor's religious thought and art. Subtle and useful.

Stanford, Donald E., editor. *The Poems of Edward Taylor.* New Haven: Yale University Press, 1960. The standard edition of Edward Taylor, though selective; prints 217 *Meditations, God's Determinations,* eleven miscellaneous poems, and brief excerpts from the *Metrical History.*

Warren, Austin. "Edward Taylor's Poetry: Colonial Baroque," *Kenyon Review* 3 (Summer 1941):355–71. Also in *Rage for Order: Essays in Criticism* (Chicago: University of Chicago Press, 1948), 1–18. A sensitive and suggestive critical appraisal of Taylor's debt to baroque conventions.

Weathers, Willie T. "Edward Taylor: Hellenistic Puritan," *American Literature* 18 (March 1946):18–26. A rare look at Taylor's reliance upon the non-English classical poetry found in his library.

Wright, Nathalia. "The Morality Tradition in the Poetry of Edward Taylor," *American Literature* 18 (March 1946):1–18. *God's Determinations* as a morality play; still excellent as an insight into the medieval character of Taylor's imagination.

Index